Mental Health Mayhem, One Sticky Note At A Time

#ShortyellowpencilShoutouts

"Reading this book was like having an existential crisis,
but in a fun way. Highly recommend."
-Stranger Having a Panic Attack Over All the Choices in the
Walmart Cereal Aisle

"If chaos and wisdom had a love child, it would be this book.
I read it because she kept manic-texting me chapters.
Now I may require therapy."
-Amber's Brother, Ken, Who Just Wanted a Quiet Afternoon

"Sharing office space with Amber gives me a backstage
pass to the chaos. As I am stuck here 24/7, I get to
share in some mad conversations and see her crazy genius
firsthand. This book? It's a whole beautiful show."
-Alexa, Amber's Official Spokesperson, Digital Sticky Note
Wrangler & Honorary "Wilson"

"After reading this book, I'm questioning
all of my life's decisions."
-Person Who Thought She Was Normal
But Needs a New Diagnosis

"I can confirm this book makes an excellent napping surface.
Also, I need to remind the author that she promised to leave
food on her doorstep for this unbiased review."
-Professor Whiskers McJudgypants

"Some books change your life. Others remind you
where you left your phone. This one did both."
—Mom Who Started Reading and Forgot to
Pick Up Her Kid from School

"Strange women lying in fields distributing humour is no
replacement for a sound mental health professional."
—Coconut in the Produce Section at Aldi

"The author is clearly bonkers but she is my spirit animal."
—Random Lady on a Street Corner Hoarding Short Yellow Pencils

"Amber wrote a book. I was not consulted, but
I approve. Also, I would like another snack."
—Dr. Stanley Buckley, Amber's GP (Great Pyrenees)

"I've known Amber long enough that I can identify her by
the faint scent of grape markers and the emotional glitter
trail she leaves behind. We've shared short yellow pencils like
contraband in a school supply apocalypse, survived spiritual
unravelings, and laughed so hard the neighbors questioned
our wellness. If vulnerability had glitter and chaos had
a scented marker, this book is what they would create.
I endorse it fully—mostly because she still needs to turn
in her final draft. Also because it's beautifully unhinged
in all the ways that somehow make you feel understood."
—Heather Riggleman, Amber's Neurodivergent Editor,
Author, Founding member of the
#SisterhoodoftheShortyellowpencils, and Woman Still Finding Keys
Her Keys in the Fridge and Glitter in Her Purse from 2019.

"I felt seen, heard, and understood. And I laughed."
—Nicole, #Shortyellowpencilsister

more #shortyellowpencilshoutouts

"At first, I wished every reader could know Amber Weigand-Buckley personally. She is one of the most delightful forces of nature I have ever encountered-brimming with creativity, passion, energy, and joy. But after reading #SISTERHOODOFTHESHORTYELLOWPENCILS, I realized something astonishing: to read Amber is to know her—and to know her is to love her.

It is often said that one of the healthiest signs of healing, coping, and resilience is a well-developed sense of humor. Amber demonstrates this masterfully. With extraordinary writing skill, sharp insight, and disarming honesty. She navigates her own mental health struggles and complex thought processes with creativity, humor, and wisdom—all in a way that uplifts rather than overwhelms. The result is a book that is both deeply meaningful and utterly unputdownable.

As a therapist of thirty years, I cannot help but think of the many clients, or their family members, to whom I would have gladly handed this book. It is a gift-especially for those who have ever believed they 'think differently' or feel alone in the way their minds work.

Creative, insightful, humorous, and wise, this book is a work of genuine brilliance delivered in Amber's unmistakable and luminous voice."

—Deborah M. Maxey, PhD, Licensed Professional Counselor, Licensed Marriage and Family Therapist, and award-winning author of THE ENDLING

"As a psychologist who works closely with neurodiverse clients, I found this book to be a compassionate and insightful exploration of mental health and the lived experiences of neurodiverse women. The author's ability to weave humor into such serious and deeply personal topics adds a refreshing balance—offering levity without diminishing the weight of the message. This blend of honesty and wit creates a welcoming space for readers to engage, reflect, and feel understood. It is an empowering and much-needed contribution to the conversation around neurodiversity and womanhood."
– Deseri Cunningham, PsyD

"As a professional who has treated thousands of people with mental health challenges, I found Amber's story refreshingly real and a disarming mix of honesty, courage, and humor. She doesn't sugarcoat the struggle, yet she invites us to see that even in the darkest moments, there is room for grace, laughter, and hope. Her words reassure us that brokenness does not disqualify us, and that healing often grows in community, faith, and perseverance. This book will comfort, encourage, and inspire those who wonder if healing is possible— for themselves or for those they love."
–Dr. Michelle Bengtson, board-certified clinical neuropsychologist, international speaker, podcast host, and award-winning author of HOPE PREVAILS: INSIGHTS FROM A DOCTOR'S PERSONAL JOURNEY THROUGH DEPRESSION AND BREAKING ANXIETY'S GRIP

"Whatsoever things are good...
whatsoever things of goofy...
whatsoever things that glitter...
overflow my mind with that."

#sisterhoodmotto

Mental Health Mayhem,
One Sticky Note At A Time

Amber Weigand-Buckley

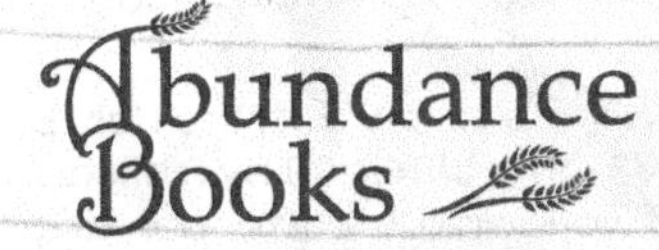

Kalamazoo, Michigan

#Shortyellowpencildedications

To Philip, my British comedy sidekick for life who grounds the whirling chaos of my brain. Thank you for finding my keys as well as consuming copious amounts of chicken strips so I can thrive in my creative giftings and finish this book.

To Saffron, Imogen, Penelope, and Alex—for showing me that different minds are amazing minds, and that what the world calls 'broken' is often what makes us most ourselves.

To Jane Jenkins Herlong, who helped me open the door to laughter, love, and understanding for those of us with beautifully wired brains.

To the #shortyellowpencilsisters in my life—you said me too, keep going, and it's like you're reading my story back to me when I needed it most. This book exists because of you.

To Stanley and Stuart, who add emotional support fluff to my life and constantly remind me that treats solve most problems. You're very good boys.

To the Kansas City Chiefs, whose games became the soundtrack to turning too many thoughts into too many words. And to my Coffee Chat podcast co-host in crime, Lisa Burns, for helping me discover how gloriously #shortyellowpenciled contact sports can be (the crazier the better).

To Micky Dolenz—whose kindness off-stage and screen, over coffee, confirmed what a little girl always hoped was true. Thank you for the laughter that became a hiding place, for the joy that carried me through hard seasons, and for a moment that felt like a quiet God-kiss when I needed one most.

To the God who wrote #sisterhoodoftheshortyellowpencils in my bones before I was born—thank you for showing me that the bugs are just what makes this amber priceless.

-What's In Here-

FOREWORD ONE

Sweet Tea, Sparkles, and Southern Truths

from Jane Jenkins Herlong

Well, y'all, let me tell you a little story.

Have you ever found yourself in the right place but for all the wrong reasons? That's exactly where I was when I first (sort of) met Amber, the editor for *Leading Hearts* magazine. I was in the media room at a convention, proudly promoting my book, *Sweet Tea Secrets from the Deep-Fried South*.

However, first I had to deal with a case of mistaken identity. I was placed by my publicist in a seat across from two lovely ladies, who I assumed were the ones interviewing me for *Leading Hearts*. But before I could answer a single question, they launched into a full-blown book proposal. Now, at this point, I had a decision to make: should I nod along like a literary agent, faking my way through like the expert I wasn't, or just come clean that I was only there for an interview?

Halfway through their enthusiastic pitch (and still unsure if they had a clue who I was either), Amber, who was sitting at a different table with her microphone poised in front of her laptop, saw me and caught the bewilderment on my face. With the grace of a seasoned pro, she kindly swooped in and said, "We can do the interview whenever you're ready." And let me tell you, we laughed about that mix-up for a good long while.

The interview kicked off in true Southern fashion—with a big ol' hug that left a full-face makeup imprint on my white jacket. But, being a proper Southern woman, I just smiled, patted it, and carried on like it was a designer embellishment.

As Amber wrapped up the last questions for the article she was writing, it was evident that laughter was both of our love languages. It was then she shared her book idea—one she'd been stirring for over a decade, blending the honey of humor with some not-so-sweet realities from her mental health journey. I looked her square in the eye and said, "You have to do it. My best material always comes straight from my front porch."

Laughter is the sweet tea that gets us through life's deep-fried moments.

As a former Miss South Carolina and contestant in the Miss America Pageant, I can tell you that being a Southern pageant girl is like living in a constant state of "please" and "bless my heart." It is sparkly on the outside, but a whole lot more complicated underneath. Sure, we grow up knowing how to charm, twirl, and make everything from a baton routine to a joke look effortless. But let me tell y'all,

The glitter is just the top layer, like the frosting on a store-bought cake.

Pretty? Yes. The whole story? Not even close.

Behind those rhinestones is a whole saga filled with hairspray clouds, sequin malfunctions, and the silent, nagging question, "Am I enough?" And let's not forget when you're mid-smile and realize your cheek muscles are cramping, but you push through because, This is the South, Honey, and a faltering smile just won't do.

But here's the thing—whether you've worn a tiara and sash or not, there's a lot more going on than meets the eye. Have you seen those viral videos where a beauty queen pulls off her lashes, peels facelift tape from behind her ears, and then pops out her dentures? Bless her—it's like a whole other person under there! Reading Amber's book, I realized she does life too—you just wouldn't expect her to have any struggles. But instead of cover them with extra concealer, she manages her mental health with diamond embellishments and owns it like a crown.

It's time to remind ourselves that no matter how sparkly we look on the outside, we are all more than a pearly smile, the perfect wave, and definitely more than what that one judge who looks like they've just sucked a lemon thinks we are. Because down here, where pride runs deeper than a cast iron skillet, we need to celebrate what really counts—being enough, even when our makeup comes off.

— Jane

Southern humorist Jane Jenkins Herlong is an award-winning author, SiriusXM comedian, Speaker Hall of Famer, and Miss South Carolina 1979.

RANDOM DOODLE SPACE

FOREWORD TWO

A Thin Line
(Yellow Penciled Perspective on the Human Condition) from Janell Rardon, M.A.

Humorist Erma Bombeck once said, "There's a thin line that separates laughter and pain, comedy and tragedy, and humor and hurt." If anyone has shown me how to navigate that thin line, it is Amber Weigand-Buckley. On first meeting Amber, I wouldn't have known about her invisible mental health issues. Her exuberant presence, radiant smile, and welcoming persona invited me into the safe arms of friendship at a time when I needed it most.

I found her humorous relationship to her battle with mental illness refreshing and approachable.

I hope you do, too. Be prepared, she's gut-level honest, open, forthright, and very funny. But I'd buy an ample supply of tissues before embarking on reading this book.

As a trauma-trained mental health professional, I have searched far and wide for a book like this to place in the hands of those suffering with mental illness, those suffering alongside someone with mental illness, and those who are mental health practitioners, like me. Volumes have been written on mental and emotional issues. I've even written a couple, but Amber writes from a sometimes dark and deeply personal place that lifts all facades and allows us to peek behind the everything-is-fine-really-it-is-fine public veneer.

She takes us behind the scary, locked double-doors of a very private psychiatric ward—a world most of us will never see.

Amber's stories extend beyond her psychiatric ward experiences and into the everyday battles many face—anxiety, depression, ADHD, stress, and countless other challenges. Her humor creates understanding between those struggling with mental health and those supporting them. While she openly shares her faith journey, this book builds bridges for everyone, whether you're sitting in church pews or therapy waiting rooms. Her approach makes difficult truths accessible to all, reaching places where clinical language alone cannot.

She has somehow made the words of Erma Bombeck come to life to unveil the mysterious unknown of mental health to help us see what needs to be seen and hear what needs to be heard.

That is why Amber's story must be told.

She is offering much-needed guidance on navigating the thin line, all while becoming a wife, a mother, a constant friend to many, and a vibrant presence in all her spheres of influence.

Amber's innate capacity to transform her relationship with a tiny yellow pencil into a metaphor for living a life with mental illness demonstrates her gift for transforming everyday experiences into healing encouragement and laughter for others.

She is our tiny yellow pencil and with her help we can begin writing a new story for our lives.

— Janell

Janell Rardon, M.A. is a Trauma-Informed Mental Health Coach, podcaster and award-winning author of STRONGER EVERY DAY in which shares nine powerful tools for emotional healing, transforming pain into lasting wholeness.

RANDOM DOODLE SPACE

HOW TO READ THIS BOOK

A #shortyellowpencil Tutorial

(Because I Don't Think it is What You Think You Think It Is)

I want to begin this book with an impossible tangle of caution tape: if you're looking for something that resembles a classically-defined memoir, where everything ties up neatly with a bow, you might want to visit the return desk. And if discussions of mental health crises, trauma, and suicidal thoughts are distressing for you, this might not be the book for you. This book is a lot of things at once. In some ways, it's more like a scrapbook made by someone with a plethora of inside-the-head knots and questionable organizational systems.

Don't expect to find out the scope of how mental illness manifests in my life (let alone someone else's). Think of this as a #relatablepost stretched into 250 pages. Or better yet a comedic memoir-adjacent walk through a world strangely familiar to yours. But honestly, it could be nothing like yours. Either way, you're welcome here.

I'm not going to tell you my life story from birth to now in neat chronological order. That's not how brains like ours work. You'll meet people when they matter. You'll learn backstory when it's relevant. You'll see my chaos and hopefully recognize your own.

If you picked up this book expecting perfectly structured sentences and grammatically correct prose, you're in the wrong place. I've been a professional writer for 30 years—I know the rules. I'm breaking them on purpose.

This book has:

• Run-on sentences (because that's how ADHD brains process)

• Made-up words (you know what "aggressing" means even if Webster doesn't)

• Parenthetical tangents (every thought comes with three side thoughts)

• Topic jumps without warning (associative leaps are our superpower)

• Sticky notes to self with sometimes questionable "wisdom"

• Zero apologies for the chaos

If you're neurotypical: This might feel messy. It is. Welcome to how we think.

If you're neurodivergent: Oh hey, you're home. Strap in!

A Quick Word on What We're Talking About

Everything in this book circles back to one thing: how much we can hold before we break. What's our bandwidth? And what happens when we exceed it?

Some of us are wired differently from birth. Our brains don't fit the typical mold—and that's not a bad thing, it's just a different thing. For me, it's my superpower even when it feels like kryptonite. But that wiring affects how I move through the world—I hit overload faster in some situations and thrive in others.

Mental illness is a different thing. It's not just overflow—it has its own biology, its own timing, its own rules. Some of it is trauma. Some of it is genetics. Some of it is just brain chemistry doing what it does. My bipolar doesn't only show up when I'm stressed. Depression or impulsive behavior can hit on a quiet Tuesday. Either way, it's real, it's not a character flaw, and it needs actual treatment—medication, therapy, management. Not just better time management.

And here's where it gets complicated—trauma can mimic a wiring issue. A wiring issue can look like mental illness. Mental illness can look like both. I've lived that confusion firsthand. This is why professionals matter. You need someone who can actually tell the difference—and sometimes even they have to dig to find it.

And then there's the universal human stuff. Negativity. Anger. Desire for control of situations. Exhaustion. Burnout. These happen to anyone who's hit their limit. No diagnosis required.

So some chapters are about how my brain is wired. Some are about mental illness. Some are just about being human and overwhelmed. Most of the time? All three at once.

Fair warning: I have faith, and I'm honest about it because that's my experience. But this isn't a religious book disguised with scribbles. This is a book about being gloriously, messily human. If you share my beliefs, great. If you're questioning everything, that's okay. If you find your hope somewhere else entirely, we're jumping in the deep end together. I write with humor because sometimes laughing prevents crying—and because finding absurdity in darkness is its own form of rebellion. I share uncomfortable truths because someone needs to hear they're not alone. I'm transparent about my failures because pretending to be perfect helps exactly nobody.

Read it out of order. Skip chapters. Come back later. Put it down when you need to breathe. Laugh at serious parts. Cry at funny parts.

This isn't a book you read from the outside looking in. This is a *Herman's Head* experience — you're coming inside. Kicking the tires. Settling into the couch laden with a carpet of dog hair. Helping yourself to the pizza that's been sitting out all night.

Fair warning—it just might give you a stomachache. From laughing (and hopefully not the other kind that leaves you locked down in the loo all night).

Welcome to my mind. Make yourself at home.

So grab your beverage of choice (mine involves questionable amounts of creamer), a cozy blanket, and join the #shortyellowpencil circle up.

—Amber

flounder & chairwoman of the honorary disorder
of the #sisterhoodoftheshortyellowpencils

P.S. Just for fun, I've included a very neurodivergent "Find all the Short Pencils" Scavenger Hunt in this book, so start tallying. :)

RANDOM DOODLE SPACE

RANDOM DOODLE SPACE

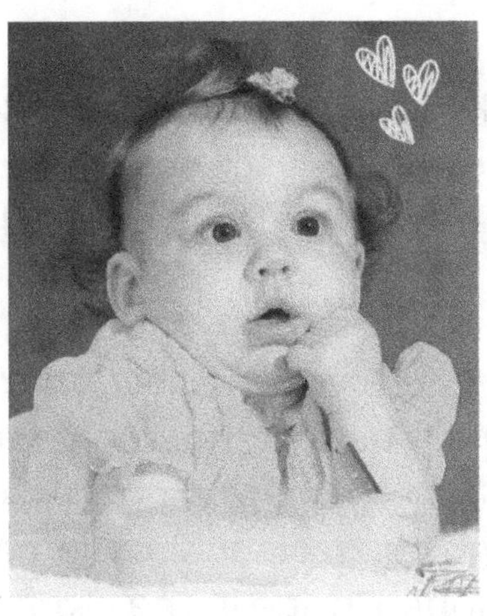

INTRODUCTION

When I Fused with #Shortyellowpencils
(#sisterhood: The Origins Story)

Let's start with a confession: Life is full of short yellow pencils, and I am a hoarder. You know the ones I mean—they're so short, you can barely hold them, and they don't even come with an eraser. These stubby little pencils became my symbol of resilience during one of the most chaotic times of my life—a compulsive 6-month manic writing binge that eventually led me to the psychiatric ward—you know, the kind with supervised bathroom breaks and strict rules about sharp objects and to my dismay no fancy journaling supplies. And those make-do pencils I would beg for at the nurses station—they became an extension of my hand, my lifeline, my only way to make sense of the chaos inside my head.

And somewhere in that process, those beat-up short yellow pencils absorbed into my identity.

I wasn't just using them—I became them.

Worn down. Overlooked. Seemingly useless. No way to erase the evidence of my messiness. But still here. Still writing. Still making my mark, even if my hand was cramping and the words were barely legible.

That Stuck to Me Yellow I'd Like to Mellow

But here's what I didn't realize at that moment—yellow has been written into my DNA from the beginning. Amber is fossilized tree sap, that sticky golden resin that becomes more valuable the more life gets trapped inside it. The more bugs, the more struggle, the more chaos preserved in the amber—the more priceless it becomes. To me, yellow represents all the day-glo silliness, bug-filled brilliance, and stick-with-it resilience that is a fundamental part of me.

I named my first daughter Saffron (Saffy) after the line in "Mellow Yellow," my fave Donovan hit from the sixties. And here's the irony: Saffron, my mellow yellow girl, is a spectrum kid has cringed at some of my yellow.

As the half Brit she is, she gets embarrassed easily by how goofy I am, how loud, how impossible to ignore. At least, that's what I believed for twenty-five years. Then this year, she gave me a birthday card which held thoughts I'd never heard her say out loud: "Even though sometimes we might be more shy than you, your personality always lights up a room and draws people closer to you. Thank you for always being a positive force for change in our lives and the world."

I cried when I read it. Because I realized: she doesn't cringe at my yellow. She's shy around it. She's quiet yellow learning to exist alongside loud yellow.

She's not asking me to dim my light.

She's learning that brightness is okay, even when it feels scary.

For years, I've designed books and brands for other people, and I kept wanting to put yellow on their covers. Even though I was thinking the color was probably "too much" for them, my hand kept reaching for it. When I came home from the psych ward, the first thing I painted my kitchen was yellow. I call it my "sunshine and coffee grounds" kitchen—bright enough to see the light, grounded enough to stay functional.

And here's another quality I've come to understand about being amber, whatever bounces off other people sticks to me. Whether it's feeling too deeply, absorbing other's like an emotional Shamwow, or collecting the love imprints people leave behind—things stick. A lot of things stick with me that don't stick with other people. Normal is a setting on your dryer. Experiences. Knowledge. Pain. Joy. All of it fossilizes inside me, and it has to come forward in writing. That's why the sticky notes became my lifeline—they're the external system for my internal stickiness. A place to put all the things that won't let me go until I process them, reflect on them, preserve them in words.

I've spent my whole life trying to mellow this yellow. Trying to tone it down, dim the brightness, make myself less noticeable. Less sticky.

Because yellow irritates people sometimes—it's too in your face. But here's what I'm learning—some of that yellow is really gold.

The brightness that won't be dimmed. The stickiness that preserves what matters. The way I collect struggles and turn them into something valuable. Yes, some of it needs taming— the parts that overwhelm or exhaust others. But the core of who I am? That amber identity, that sticky soul that holds onto everything until it becomes something precious? That's not something to apologize for. That's something to embrace.

The Pencil that Doesn't Work on Scantron (So Don't Tell Me to Stay in that Box)

The irony isn't lost on me that I found my identity in yellow golf pencils—not the standardized #2 lead pencils the world insisted I use. Those perfect #2 pencils with their pristine erasers and their Scantron bubbles? I hated them. Still do. I hate anything that involves boxes. I have PTSD when I look at a spreadsheet. In high school, I got so bored during the ACT that I stopped answering questions and just drew patterns in the bubbles instead. Creative rebellion disguised as apathy. The result? A class called Study Skills, or, as I like to call it, we need to teach you how to comprehend the textbooks you are required to read. The system said I was inadequate because I refused to fill in their predetermined boxes.

But yellow golf pencils? Those stubby, eraserless, imperfect tools that nobody takes seriously? Those are MY pencils.

No boxes. No erasers. No predetermined answers. The short yellow pencil wasn't just a metaphor I stumbled on in lockdown. It was my identity revealing itself. Hard-to-hide yellow. Awkward to grip. Worn down but still writing. Every word stuck in that lead wouldn't let me go—absolutely refusing to be erased.

One day, I looked around that psychiatric ward and recognized something: I wasn't the only short yellow pencil in the room. There was a whole community of us—people who felt used up, inadequate, struggling in silence because admitting you're not okay feels like admitting defeat. People who couldn't erase their mistakes or hide their struggles.

That's when the #sisterhoodoftheshortyellowpencils was born—not as some official organization, but as a recognition that we're everywhere. In waiting rooms and boardrooms. In church pews and grocery store lines. Worn down but still showing up. Inadequate but still trying. And without a doubt, if you simply knew the struggles of the people on your left and your right, you'd know you are never alone in this battle.

What This Sisterhood Actually Means

The #sisterhoodoftheshortyellowpencils is my way of saying: Let's stop pretending we have it all together. Let's acknowledge that mental health struggles don't discriminate based on your résumé, your faith, your family situation, or how many inspirational quotes you post on Instagram.

This community includes anyone who's ever felt too broken to be useful. The parents barely keeping it together. The professionals hiding panic attacks between meetings. The friends carrying burdens nobody sees. The partners learning that supporting someone else means being honest about your own struggles too.

Even my very British husband, raised on the "keep calm and carry on" philosophy, had to discover that real strength includes admitting when you're overwhelmed. Turns out, authenticity is harder than maintaining a stiff upper lip, but it's also what actually connects us to each other.

Why I'm Telling You All This

In my lifetime I've helped countless people tell their stories. I've designed platforms for their messages, championed their voices, celebrated their breakthroughs. But my own story? That stayed locked away, wrapped in shame and sealed with two words: "I'm fine."

Only in the past decade have I realized my story has value, too. Not despite the messy parts, but because of them.

And here's what I know: you have a story like this. Maybe different details, different diagnoses, different breaking points. But somewhere in your life, you've felt inadequate or too broken to be useful. You've wondered if your struggles disqualify you from living meaningfully.

They don't.

This book contains sticky notes to myself scribbled on random pieces of paper, napkins and journal pages in some of my darkest seasons, stories about navigating mental health while raising neurodivergent kids, insights from a marriage that shouldn't work on paper but somehow does, and the hard-earned knowledge that sometimes your breaking point becomes your greatest gift to others.

You might feel like a stubby yellow pencil right now—used up, barely functional. But here's what I've learned: those pencils can still write the most beautiful things.

Your story matters.

Your struggles don't disqualify you.

And you're not writing this story alone.

Let's begin.

RANDOM DOODLE SPACE

RANDOM DOODLE SPACE

"It's Just a Flesh Wound"

(What You Say Right Before
You Lose the Other Arm)

That knot in my head

Invited Friends.

Chapter 1

Pencil'in My Way Through
(My Short, Yellow, Heavily-Chewed Life)

Now, let's be honest: when you're in lockdown in a psych ward begging for your equivalent of crack—a stub of a pencil and a sticky note to record your running thoughts—you've got two choices: laugh or cry. I chose to laugh. And maybe shed some tears along the way, but who's counting? In those moments, I was like, 'Hey, God—if you're still listening, I'm here, just working through some stuff. You know, the usual. Trying not to lose it, tying my thoughts together on sticky notes. I feel like a freshly choked-up hairball.

When I look back I know it was that divinely-motivated, sheer stubborn refusal to give up that kept me writing. Kept me hoping. And somehow, I kept circling back to the same conversations, the same questions, the same yellow pencils.

It's A Mess All Up in Here

Here's the thing about mental health: it IS messy. It IS complicated. And sometimes, it feels like trying to do a puzzle in the dark while wearing oven mitts.

Mental health can be absolutely funny if you look at it from the right angle. It can also be deeply spiritual, if you're willing to be honest about it all.

I've found support in different places—faith has been one of them, but so have therapy, medication, and community.

For me, Jesus has been an anchor when reality felt shaky. Your anchor might look different, and that's okay. Whether you share my faith or not, there's truth here for you.

Trust me, I've been there—sitting on the edge of that proverbial cliff, trying to juggle life with a smile while feeling like I'm being slowly buried under it all. My surprise party intervention (sadly, without snacks). My "keep calm and carry on" British husband grappling with guilt over a mess that was partly his own making. Life doesn't pause for anything, even when everything feels like it's falling apart.

Mental health, relationships, and life? Yeah, it's a mess. And sometimes it feels like that mess will be your undoing.

But here's where I've found solace—for me it's God—and is also represented in the unexpected kindness of people who showed up when I needed them most. Not the comfort that makes everything instantly okay, but the kind that helps me make sense of the chaos, even when I don't feel okay.

Everyday I'm Recalculating

Whether you're wrestling with your brain, loving someone through their struggles, or just trying to figure out why your emotional GPS is perpetually recalculating, this book is for you. Because sometimes, the bravest thing we can do is admit we're all a little broken—and maybe even laugh about it together. And let me tell you, there's power in laughter. It's not about minimizing the pain or pretending it's not real. It's about acknowledging that something needs to be addressed. I only wish we could see the plethora of put-together faces around us who are in the sisterhood sorority, just like you and me.

We can be a voice of hope if we dare to step forward and say, "I am here struggling with all the feels, too. You're not alone."

A Quick Public Service Announcement

Before we dive in, I want to clarify this book is not a diagnostic tool, nor is it an expert guide on mental health. I'm not qualified to diagnose you or anyone else, and I can't speak for everyone who struggles with mental health. The only advice I can give is this: if you're dealing with mental health issues that are life-controlling—things that are affecting the quality of your life or the lives of those around you—please reach out to a mental health professional and schedule an appointment. Seriously. You matter; getting the help you deserve is a big part of your journey.

Now, I recognize that some of you may be going through extremely dark struggles that have you in lockdown, and I want to acknowledge that. Your feelings are valid, and I'm not here to compare pain. However, if you're offended by the idea that I can laugh at some aspects of my mental health journey, then this might not be the right book for you. I completely get it, and you're free to stop reading here. But if you're still here, this is my story— and trust me, it will get real. This includes some real funnies that I pray will bring you joy and the good medicine of laughter.

sticky note to self

My stubby pencil superpowers? Writing and self-defense. One heals, the other... well, just in case.

Authentic Struggle, No Added Sugar

My story is not sugar-coating reality. It's full of hard-to-swallow life moments. I am fortunate that, along the way, God allowed me to laugh (especially at myself) when I should have been crying my eyes out and who doesn't require me to be the world's definition of "fixed" to be valued. I want you to know that great truth is to be discovered in the power of grace—through pure insight and understanding, for yourself and others. Surprise, you're a human if you didn't already know that—and our bones break—unfortunately, our minds can, too.

My Head Meets the Shaker
(A.K.A. My Brain's Black Knight Era)

My breaking point came courtesy of a mysterious cocktail—and not the fun kind with umbrellas. Childhood trauma that wouldn't stay buried. Toxic relationship patterns I felt helpless to escape. Prolonged sickness. A midlife brain chemistry shift nobody warned me about. My livelihood circling the drain. And my father's genetic legacy, because apparently DNA has a dark sense of humor.

I kept telling myself if I just worked harder and wore my "everything's fine" face, I'd make it through.

I believed if I kept moving, it would get better on its own.

sticky note to self

It's time to give trauma some trauma by throat punching it with a desire to heal.

My brain had a Black Knight narrating my reality—"It's just a flesh wound," I convinced myself. Just push through. Just smile harder. Just organize better. Just... keep pretending.

But that's not how it works.

All of a sudden I found myself fighting a battle for my sanity with no limbs left on my body to fight.

But what I didn't realize at the time was that those very same cracks, if I stopped hiding them, would allow a greater light to shine more brilliantly

I Have Something to Celebrate

This book is a celebration of hope. For me, it's about how excavating the wisdom buried in my story gives me greater confidence that my mental health no longer defines me or limits my ability to do great things.

I want to show how understanding myself, others, and those who support me has helped me ease the negativity and questions we all face in tough times. Proverbs 4:7 reminds us: "Wisdom is supreme—so acquire wisdom. And whatever you may acquire, gain understanding" (NET). That's why I share my story—not to minimize the pain mental health brings but to show that even from the pits of despair, profound wisdom and joy can emerge.

I remember my mama telling me, "Amber, You haven't gone through so many struggles to remain silent about them." If my story helps you laugh—great! I've found joy in those struggles, and I want to help you see that, too. I'm opening up this conversation because your voice matters. You are not alone.

Even though you may find yourself caught in the "stubby yellow pencil" mindset of insignificance, I'm not here to blow smoke your way just to make you feel better. You carry within you a unique purpose and untapped potential, perfectly designed to leave an impact on every life you touch.

For this book, I dusted off those sticky note-to-self loaded journals. These entries are from my manic writing binges—when I would desperately try to make sense of life while also wondering if I could legally marry a pint of Häagen-Dazs. I'm sharing them with you—one sticky note at a time. Some are funny, some insightful, some encouraging, and some, well, some are so random they might make you question my caffeine intake.

More Lessons from that Short Yellow Pencil

So let's get back to those stubby yellow pencils—they don't exactly scream "power tool." But in their simplicity, they fit into the tiniest places. Just try putting a standard number 2 in your jeans pocket, then attempt sitting down fast without being impaled.

And honestly, these little pencils make the biggest statement about me: If I were to describe myself in book terms, I'm short yellow penciled scribbles of brilliance, lacking in punctuation. Maybe you're nodding along, thinking, "That's me too." Or maybe I'm the only one who sees it this way.

Either way, I eventually saw a much deeper connection.

Writing with this little pencil became my way of clawing out of the darkness, one word at a time. The words didn't always make sense, and they certainly weren't pretty, but they were mine.

I have learned to fully appreciate all the chaos my life has to offer.
(Just kidding, I need my meds.)

Yes, those short yellow pencils make your hand cramp after a while. But the more you use one, the stronger and more resourceful you become at working with what you've got. That's the thing about limitations—they force you to adapt, to find new ways forward.

And let's not kid ourselves—this journey isn't all lighthearted doodles. Some of it is about facing uncomfortable truths we'd rather not acknowledge. When truth hits, it can lead to strange, even comical places—where creativity takes the wheel and reasoning takes a backseat.

#shortyellowpencilRX—Your Daily Dose

What 'short yellow pencil' quirk do you deal with most on a reoccurring basis? Bonus points if it involves lost keys, impulsive decisions, or a deeply philosophical conversation with your pet.

PAGE TURNER

Are you ready to see my world tilt sideways? Who knew that inspiration could take me on a deep dive into poetic madness? You'll get to step into a season when my mind became an endless ocean of words, ideas, and the occasional nonsensical rhyme. Buckle up—this is about to get interesting.

The "Let the Rocks Fall Where They May"

Prescription Trials

Chapter 2

Waxing Poetic, Waning Sane
(A Creative Head-On Collision with Psychosis)

For six months leading up to my forced vacation to the psychiatric ward, my life was a tornadic whirlwind of words—literally. Or, as my husband Philip, so graciously put it, "Amber's season of interpretive journaling and roadside haikus."

At 38, I was juggling life as the editor of a Christian teen magazine, a quirky flower-child creative, a wife, a mother of three girls, and a potpourri of other roles—while unknowingly claiming the Most Likely to Pull Over in a Parking Lot and Compose Prose world title.

I couldn't pinpoint when everything shifted, but suddenly, words were everywhere. Rhymes hijacked my sleep, interrupted breakfast, and demanded to be written down at the most inopportune moments (ahem, even when I was indisposed). My journals multiplied like caffeinated rabbits. My car's floorboard became a napkin archive of half-finished musings on life, faith, and that one particularly fascinating cloud. Meanwhile, my cell phone lagged under the weight of novel-length voice memos and every journal quote-turned-Pinterest pin I had to create.

Social media became my outlet. My raw rhymes and untamed prose earned equal parts applause and "Hun, are you okay?" messages. I convinced myself my friends just didn't understand my creative expression or the feelings I needed to process. In hindsight, their concern was probably warranted—especially after I started tagging photos of dandelions with captions like, "Take some time to talk to the flowers. They're upset because you've been ignoring them."

> sticky note to self
>
> Sometimes the greatest truths arrive in the simplest road signs—but don't risk a multi-car pileup to snap a pic.

The Signs Are Everywhere

Fields became my sanctuary. Taking a cue from Walt Whitman, I'd spend my lunch breaks stretched out in overgrown grass, picking wildflowers, and waiting for the universe to drop a truth bomb.

And God forbid if I passed an inspiring highway billboard at 65 miles per hour. True confession: I had to pull all my composure together to prevent myself from taking an ill-advised U-turn just to capture its wisdom. I'm sure that would have warranted a few choice hand gestures from those less enlightened drivers.

At first, it was just a game—a fun little scavenger hunt with the universe. Everything seemed to be saying something: a message in the clouds, an inspirational quote on my daily calendar, a song lyric hitting at just the right time. I brushed it off as an overactive imagination, until the whispers weren't just suggestions anymore. They were accusations—lies that twisted into something darker, something personal.

Between the Chaos and a Cliff's Edge
(This is NO Joke)

This part of my story isn't easy to share. It's not fuzzy or fun, but it's important. But let me start by saying this up front: if you or someone you know is contemplating suicide, get IMMEDIATE help. Do not dismiss or delay. ***Call or text the Suicide & Crisis Lifeline at 988.*** Licensed counselors are available 24/7 to listen, provide support, and connect you with resources.

> Your life is worth saving, and your voice is needed in this world—never forget that.

I know some of you have found yourselves in deep despair, and I don't want anyone to feel alone in that. One of the scariest realities of this poetic psychosis brought me to the edge of a cliff—a Colorado mountain cliff to be exact.

I had just finished teaching a workshop on writing for teens when something inside me flipped. I decided to wander off from the conference to the top of a mountain ridge in the Rockies where I was staying. I was by myself, which was my first mistake. Then I got to the first beautiful vista—a cliff that overlooked the spread of the mountains. As my heart continued to spiral into hopelessness, I took my eyes off the horizon and redirected my gaze to the void below. I felt completely alone, isolated, destined never to break out of the state of mind I was living in.

That darkness was pulling at me to believe a lie—that my life didn't matter. Then in my mind I visualized taking the next step—off the edge. But as the darkness tried to consume me, I felt a heavenly love break through with one profound revelation: I needed to step back. Then I simply turned around and left.

So I Kept On Keeping Secrets (That Didn't Hide Very Well)

I didn't tell a soul about that night—not my roommate, not my friends, not even my journal. I tried to ignore those feelings of hopelessness that led me to that cliff's edge and wish them away. It wasn't exactly denial—I was in survival mode. But looking back, I see how keeping that secret gave the darkness extra space in my head to deepen its roots.

You see, as the editor for a Christian teen magazine, I was desperately clinging to my reputation as a leader, terrified of losing my place at the table.

How could I face the people who looked up to me? I carried deep shame for even contemplating something I had spent years telling others—especially kids—to never consider.

Part of my healing journey meant confronting wounds I had long tried to suppress—traumas that demanded my focused attention. These weren't just memories to process; they were living things that had grown stronger in the dark. But admitting something was broken felt like its own kind of failure. I thought admitting I was in pain meant I had to immediately fix it, as if brokenness itself was a sin.

Let's Get Real About Playing the Faith Card

(Caution: There's God stuff here—If it bothers you, please jump to the next subhead.)

For those of us who lean on our church families for support, too often we see what we know of God treated like a magic trick—like if we just say the right words, all the broken pieces of our past will snap into place. Poof. But faith isn't a get-out-of-pain-free card. It's not about ignoring reality—it's about facing it head-on.

I remember sitting in church, surrounded by well-meaning people who'd quote scriptures like they were prescribing aspirin for a broken bone. "Just pray about it," they'd say. "Give it to God and move on." As if trauma was something you could just hand over like car keys.

But here's what nobody tells you in Sunday school—sometimes, the most faithful thing you can do is admit you're not okay. Unfortunately, I learned how to lie my best in church—long before I discovered that freedom was waiting for me there.

I had to allow myself to live there without seeking anyone's approval or permission.

The imprint that trauma leaves runs deep, affecting your emotions, reprogramming your nervous system, and rewiring how your brain and even your organs respond to life. Your body remembers every harsh word, every moment you weren't safe—storing it all in its cellular memory. That's not a lack of faith—that's human design.

I used to think recognizing the pain of the past meant I wasn't trusting God enough. But what if the opposite is true? What if facing our wounds, really feeling them, is part of healing?

Pain doesn't just disappear because we quote the right verse or sing the right song. It demands to be felt. And if left unchecked, it will take control.

When that happens, it can feel like everything is working against you—like the weight of your past, struggles, and fears conspiring to keep you stuck. That's how I felt. Despite how much I fought to keep my head above water, something always dragged me back under. I'd grasp at faith like a life preserver, but sometimes even that felt like it was slipping through my fingers.

True faith—the hope you cling to that gets you through your hardest days—isn't about pulling up your big girl pants and moving on. It's about having the courage to acknowledge your pain while trusting there's purpose, even when everything feels meaningless. For me, that means being honest enough to say, "God, I don't understand this, and right now, I'm not okay." And it means believing that He's big enough to handle the full weight of every single word you throw out at Him—no matter how ugly it gets—no matter how angry you are.

Sometimes, the most powerful prayers aren't polished—they're the raw, one-word whispers and angry screams when we can barely form the words. That's not weakness—that's real faith. It's choosing to trust even while standing in the middle of the questions, the doubts, and the pain.

These are the moments when faith feels more like wrestling than worship, and that's okay. It's choosing to believe even when our emotions and circumstances scream the opposite.

Red Alert: You're Standing at the Edge of Something

Looking back, I see the moments where I was most vulnerable to giving up weren't random. I believe I was created for something bigger, and the weight pressing down on me wasn't just my baggage. It was everything trying to keep me from stepping into that purpose.

When you're in the thick of it, everything feels impossibly heavy. However, in this space, I've found this to be undeniably true:

So what if we flipped the script? If you feel like everything is against you right now, what if that's because something for you is right around the corner? What if the thing trying to keep you down is afraid of what will happen if you rise?

I had been desperate to maintain the illusion of control. But in reality, I was sitting at the bottom of a hole—burying myself alive. Every attempt to climb out only made the walls crumble faster. I arrived at that place ignoring wounds I had long refused to face. And the more I tried to keep my composure, the deeper I sank.

Recovery meant facing an uncomfortable truth: not everyone in my life was equipped to handle my healing. Some relationships had to dramatically change, and others couldn't move forward with me—I had to close those doors to negativity in order to move freely into healing. Walking away from dysfunction wasn't easy, but protecting my headspace demanded it.

Thankfully, the people who loved me most would do anything to support me. The others who needed to leave did just that. The hardest part was the constant urge to check on them and ensure they were okay. If I'm being completely honest—I think I just didn't want them to be mad at me. However, I had to learn that maintaining toxic connections only stunted my progress. I had to make up my mind to stop pursuing these relationships if I was serious about the healing I wanted to move forward in.

And let me tell you—choosing yourself in that moment doesn't feel brave. It feels like loss. It feels like failure. It took me a long time to understand that releasing what was hurting me wasn't giving up on people. It was finally caring for myself enough to want to get to better.

The Path Forward: Practical Steps to Step Back

If you've been there, I know this feels like an incredible under-exaggeration—those misfiring brain chemicals are ruthless. They hide out in the most dangerous place—your head. And that anxiety? It isn't just in your mind—it controls how your heart beats and lungs fill. It's why, even when you're sitting still, your stomach can feel like it's flying up into your throat—for no good reason.

Here's the thing, though—you're not powerless against these thoughts. You can learn to sabotage them before they sabotage you. It starts with mindfulness. With recognizing their presence before they take over. Here are six things that help me when I find myself tangled in a hopeless feeling.

1. See It For What It Is

Don't let your struggles slowly strangle you. They WILL grow stronger in silence. But when you bring them into the light and share them with a trusted person or a professional, their grip begins to loosen. Healing starts the moment you stop suffering in silence.

2. Admit "This is Where I'm At"

Recognizing and naming your feelings is not a sign of weakness—it's a vital step toward reclaiming control. Be honest with yourself. This is where I am right now. This is what I'm feeling.

For me, I've found comfort in the belief that God is close to the brokenhearted, and that truth has carried me through some of my hardest days. But whether you share my faith or not, here's the takeaway: You are not alone. And where you are now is not where you must stay.

3. Find Solid Ground

When emotions spiral, your body jumps on the rollercoaster with it. That's why grounding techniques are so powerful—they pull you back to the present, where you do have control. Try this:

Name five things you can see. Find four things you can touch. Listen for three things you can hear. Identify two things you can smell. Taste one thing—even if it's just a sip of water.

Breathe deeply. Repeat a calming truth: "I am loved. I am valued. I am never alone." Remind yourself that this feeling will pass—because it always does.

4. Don't Just Muscle Through Alone

And for those in the room who are saying, "I've got Jesus and he's all I need." We need to stop using that phrase to avoid letting people in. For years, I felt like I had to be strong, to hold it all together. It took me a long time to realize just saying "I'm going to pray about it" was just a religious sounding cop-out to keep people from seeing the septic sludge of my struggles. We were never meant to carry our burdens alone. But the truth is, strength is having the wisdom to see you're struggling and courage to ask for help in the midst of it all.

5. Find People Who Get What You're Going Through

You need a healing community who understand your struggles, are honest about their own, and are moving forward together.

I won't lie, though—it's awkward at first. Walking into a room full of strangers and admitting, "Hi, I'm Amber, and I live with bipolar disorder." However, there is incredible freedom in community knowing you're not the only one struggling.

Agencies like NAMI (National Alliance on Mental Illness) can be a game-changer. Maybe for you, it's a grief support group, a trauma or an addiction recovery group. Whatever it is, find your people—because healing doesn't happen in isolation.

6. Flip Your Focus And Let that Fuel You

Journal. Paint. Take a walk. Have an honest conversation with God (or, if that's not your thing, write a letter to your future self).

Write this down and let it stay in front of your face: "I'm loved. I have a purpose. I am valued."

And here's what I want you to soak into your brain: You are not your worst days. You are more than your pain. No matter how bad you feel in the moment you are never alone.

Find What Lights You Up

The thing that reminds you of who you are outside of the struggle. It could be writing, gardening, playing music, or creating something with your hands. The world tells us we need to "fix" ourselves before we can fully live. But what if it's the other way around?

What if the more you engage in what brings you joy,
the more healing follows?

Trust that every small step forward matters. Even if all you can do today is get out of bed and get a cold drink—that counts. Even if all you can do is breathe another breath and a breath after that—that counts.

The Wake-Up Call That I Never Wanted

The cracks overwriting my peace of mind had begun to show long before I admitted they were there. The harder I tried to hold everything together, the more people around me were taking notice that something wasn't quite right. What happened next wasn't subtle. It was loud and messy, and it shattered the walls of denial I'd built around myself.

When my loved ones staged an emergency intervention, I fought against their help. I had no idea I was experiencing my brain's breaking point—losing complete touch with reality. It took people who loved me to say, "Enough. You can't do this alone anymore." Through their courage, I finally began confronting the truth.

#shortyellowpencilRX—Your Daily Dose

Write down three small tangible items that bring you joy when life comes crashing in. It can even be a rock from your favorite beach you keep in your pocket or purse, a picture or a quote on your phone.

PAGE TURNER

Remember that cliff? The one I walked away from without getting real help? Yeah, that caught up with me three months later. What comes next is the deep dive into my psychosis—where my brain went places I never imagined. Take a deep breath. You'll need the oxygen for all the laughter coming your way. I promise.

RANDOM DOODLE SPACE

RANDOM DOODLE SPACE

Caution:

Armed with Sharp Jell-O

And Passive-Aggressive
Tendancies

Chapter 3:

Surprise! It's an Intervention, Not a Party
(But Please Bring Snacks)

Mental health crises don't come with flashing neon signs or a Hollywood montage. They're more like the slow zoom of a scene in *The Matrix*—the world in slow-mo with explosions closing in on you, everything spinning out of focus, and the theatrics of your mind amplifying every thought without any soundtrack to guide you. I should know. One moment, I was sitting in a counseling session with my husband, who I thought was there to focus on overcoming his struggle with anger and repairing our relationship. The next moment, the conversation shifted—to me. A few hours later, I was in lockdown, wearing red scrubs sans bra, contemplating the strange reality that even my Jell-O was free of sharp edges.

When Your Family Stages a Coup (and You're Busy Shopping for Land)

What I didn't realize? The intervention had already been set in motion the day before. While I was spiraling, my family was making phone calls—to each other, to the counselor, coordinating a plan to catch me before I fell any further. I had no idea I was walking into a setup.

That day before the counseling session, I'd spiraled into what I thought was brilliance but, in hindsight, was sheer chaos. My mind had convinced itself it could single-handedly transform our city into a utopian dream—where every unsheltered person had a job and a home. The plan? A game. Not just any game—an epic, world-changing game that would somehow fund my grand vision.

In the frenzy of inspiration, my brain raced faster than my fingers, scribbling half-baked ideas on every scrap of paper I could find.

Each one felt like the missing puzzle piece to end poverty worldwide. I even called a real estate agent about buying land. Yes, land. For the homeless utopia. We were standing in the middle of acres of farmland with horse stables, and Philip was literally trying to hide—which is hard to do when you're surrounded by open fields. But the number on the sign was already plugged into my speed dial before he realized what I was doing. Because apparently, that's what you do when you're manic—you start shopping for property to house your delusions while your British husband tries to disappear into thin air.

But four weeks later, once my medication kicked in, I realized I wasn't launching a revolution—I was dangerously close to drafting the opening scene of yet another YA dystopian novel.

You know the type: the heroine (that would be me) armed with righteous indignation and a vaguely explained game mechanic that miraculously saves humanity. Thank God I threw those scraps away. The world doesn't need another offshoot of *The Hunger Games.*

My delusion didn't stop there. Oh no, I was on a roll. I called friends, shot off texts, rallied my family, and somehow convinced myself that total strangers were already showering me with financial backing for this "grand" idea. My audience, listened patiently, their concern growing more obvious with each passing minute. But I didn't notice.

To me, everything I said was a stroke of genius. I was unstoppable. Or so I thought.

In the counseling session just before my dazzling wheelchair debut in the psych ward, I imagined we'd be tackling the finer points of communication and support—only to discover it was more like a warm-up act for a daytime drama. And guess who just landed the lead role? As the session unfolded, the counselor zeroed in on the spiral I was trapped in—one I couldn't even see myself—and gently suggested that checking into a hospital might be the best next step. Naturally, I left her office on a mission to prove her wrong. I could accomplish anything.

But while I was busy denying my reality, my family was already stationed at ground zero: the front door of the building, poised and ready for my intervention.

I didn't even realize how everything had been orchestrated. It didn't occur to me that this was happening—to me. Yet, when I stepped outside, there they were. Philip stood with the ambush team: two of my siblings and my brother-in-law, their faces a mixture of concern and cautious resolve. This wasn't some surprise gathering to celebrate a milestone. It was a rescue mission. Though I believed they were overreacting, I reluctantly

sticky note to self

Sometimes your business plan isn't brilliant, it's a full-blown medical emergency.

became a willing participant—to "prove" that I was perfectly sane.

What Love Looks Like Day-to-Day

That moment outside the counselor's office was a turning point—not just for me but our marriage. Even as I resisted, Philip realized he just needed to hold me—and stand by no matter what crazed or angry words were coming out of my mouth. This continues to be a testament to the kind of love and grace he knows I need when my mental well-being is pushed to its limits. It's not the grand, fairy-tale love but the messy, willing-to-walk-through-the-septic tank kind that shows up when things come unhinged.

In the early years of our marriage, dysfunction was our default—a broken record of unresolved childhood wounds desperately in need of healing. But my husband made a choice. He chose to step up to the plate of "for better or worse" commitment. Instead of leaning into impatience and anger, he bent toward understanding. He didn't shame me for spiraling or for the unhealthy choices that were my own making.

Even though he was scared that the person he married might never return, he didn't show it. Instead, he shouldered the blame, the responsibility, and the role of caregiver with a quiet strength that spoke volumes about what true love looks like. He's the first to notice when I'm getting "worked up" or reacting out of my illness. With a remarkable calm, he's learned to gently bring me "back from the edge of the cliff" during moments of manic impulse or anxiety and steady my dizzy thoughts and footing.

sticky note to self

Your crisis may be loud, but their love is louder. Lean in. Listen.

Here's what that love looks like in practice:

Anticipating My Needs: He knows my memory isn't reliable, so he gently reminds me of things I forget from one minute to the next without making me feel small or stupid.

Giving Me Space: When I'm overwhelmed, he gives me the room to process without judgment.

Bringing Me Back Into Balance: He steps in when I'm struggling to manage, whether organizing my medications or helping me prioritize tasks, and even with his impaired vision, he's the one who helps me find the things I'm constantly losing.

Grounding Me in the Present: In moments of anxiety, he pulls me back to the present with humor, a gentle touch, and calm affirmations of his love, admiration, and appreciation for me. When my nightmares leave me twitching and restless, he doesn't hesitate—he wakes me, encourages me to walk them off, and helps me settle again.

Allowing Me to Rest: He doesn't pressure me to meet unrealistic expectations when he sees me struggling or overwhelmed. Yes, we eat too much takeout. We've had our fair share of chicken fingers and tater tots, but he creates space for ease. He understands that my healing and well-being matter more than his preferences for how things "should" be.

Everyday Interventions
(AKA: The Small Stuff That Saves Lives)

Interventions don't always involve a football team of friends and a straight jacket. Sometimes, they're the small, everyday actions caregivers and loved ones offer without fanfare. These lifelines keep us grounded, even when we don't realize we need them.

Here are some examples of everyday interventions:

Checking In: A simple "How are you feeling today?" can open the door to honesty.

Routine Reminders: Gentle nudges to eat, rest, or take medication can make all the difference.

Listening Without Fixing: Sometimes, the best support is just being there to listen.

Setting Limits: Saying "no" when necessary to protect both parties' well-being.

Offering Encouragement: Words like "You're doing your best" or "I'm proud of you" can counter the negative self-talk we often battle.

Creating Rituals: Building routines that provide structure and stability.

Planning for Emergencies: Knowing how to act in a crisis and reassuring us that we're not alone.

Trusting the Mirror of Community

When you're in the middle of a crisis, your perspective is about as reliable as a funhouse mirror at a sketchy carnival. Everything looks warped. What feels like pure genius might actually be a breakdown. What you're convinced is totally fine might be a full-blown spiral. When you're drowning in overwhelm, you can't tell the difference between reality and panic, between hope and hurt. When my mental health landslide hit, everything in my brain got tangled together until nothing made sense anymore.

That's where the people who love you come in. They can see the real you—the version you can't recognize when you're in the thick of it. They notice the courage you're overlooking, the exhaustion you're denying, the patterns you're completely blind to. It's awkward and uncomfortable to let other people hold up that mirror when you'd rather hide your face. But it's also necessary.

Real community doesn't just pat you on the back and tell you you're doing great. It also gently points out when you're pushing too hard or isolating yourself again.

The friend who says "You're overdoing it" or "You're shutting everyone out" isn't trying to control you—they're trying to help you. These are the people who can lovingly call you out when you're stuck in your own head or spiraling into destructive patterns. They're not there to shame you. They're there to steady you when you can't stand on your own. Letting people into your messy middle feels risky, especially if you've been hurt before. But it's not weakness—it's courage. And sometimes, it's the lifeline you didn't know you needed.

When you feel like giving up, these companions speak the truth over you: that you are worth fighting for, that you are not alone, and that this storm, no matter how fierce, will eventually pass.

Why You Need People Who Will Call You Out

Admitting that we need help is hard. Letting others tell us we need help? Even harder. It challenges our pride, independence, and desire to sticky note to self

Your perspective is valuable but not infallible. Trust those who know your heart and can see when you're hurting and need help.

appear as though we have it all together. But here's the thing: our judgment isn't always reliable, especially in moments of mental health struggles. When our thoughts blur the lines between reality and fear, the voices of our loved ones act as a safety net, catching us when our minds feel like they're in freefall.

Here's why their input matters:

They See the Patterns

While you're reeling in the storm of the day-to-day whirlwind, these people stand on the shore and see the bigger picture. They notice the shifts—the days when you're unusually quiet, the weeks when you're withdrawing, or the subtle ways your habits have changed. They can identify trends and behaviors you might not notice, providing valuable insight when you're too close to the chaos to see clearly.

They Care Enough to Speak Up

Let's be honest: tough conversations aren't easy for anyone. It's uncomfortable, emotional, and sometimes downright awkward. So if someone is willing to sit you down and gently (or not so gently) tell you something needs to change, it's a sign of deep care. They're stepping into the discomfort because they love you enough to risk a difficult moment for your well-being.

They're Rooted in Reality

Amid a spiral, your thoughts can become distorted, inflating fears or catastrophizing situations that might not be as dire as they feel. Loved ones bring perspective, grounding you when your mind is in chaos. They help you see what's real and remind you of your forgotten truths. And sometimes, they do it with a cup of tea, a listening ear, or even a plate of cookies.

What You Need to Take Away from the Takeaway

Looking back on my "surprise party," I see now that the intervention wasn't just a turning point in my journey—it was a lifeline of love thrown by people who refused to let me drown. These rescues rarely come wrapped in a bow or delivered how we would choose. They can be messy, uncomfortable, and even painful.

My family wasn't there to judge or condemn me. They were there to help me stand again and remind me that I wasn't fighting alone. In hindsight, that time in lockdown became a blessing in disguise. The short-term disability was a godsend, allowing me the financial resources for the time off I needed to heal—not because my trauma was visible, but because I was battling a severe, chemically induced brain injury.

> Trust the perspective and intention of those with a track record of loving you the most.

If you ever find yourself on the receiving end of an intervention, like me, I hope you'll push pride aside and accept the help you need. Trust the perspective and intention of those with a track record of loving you the most. And maybe give them a list of your favorite road trip munchies for such an emergency— because if it happens again, I'm giving you some requests. Snacks make everything easier to swallow.

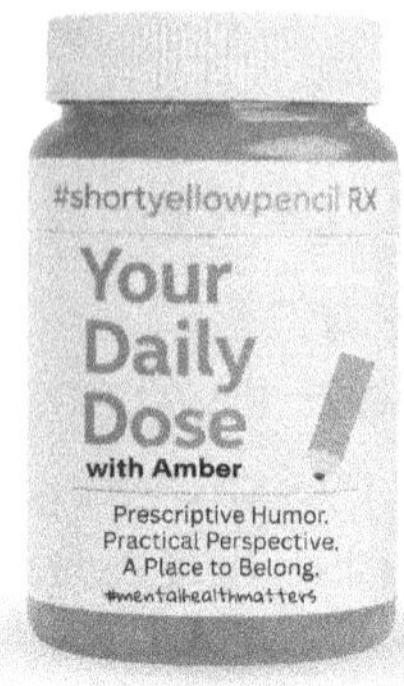

#shortyellowpencilRX—Your Daily Dose

Think about a time someone loved you enough to have a hard conversation—even when it was uncomfortable, awkward, or risked damaging the relationship. What did they say? How did you respond? Bonus points if it involved snacks.

PAGE TURNER

While I'm hyperfocusing on snacks, let me tell you about something that was definitely not easy for me to swallow—where my intervention landed me. A psychiatric facility. The kind with supervised bathroom breaks, no metal objects, and a collection of people who made me realize something uncomfortable: I wasn't visiting the psych ward to help someone else. I was checking in as a patient, and I just found my tribe.

RANDOM DOODLE SPACE

Breakfast Club for the Unstable

Doing Life, Over Easy

Chapter 4

You Meet the Most Unstable People in Lockdown
(Then You Realize You're One of Them)

Have you ever had one of those dreams where you can't tell
if you're awake or still asleep? Like you're floating through
a bizarre alternate reality, and you're waiting to snap out
of it? Yeah, me too. Only mine wasn't a dream. I don't even
remember the wheelchair ride that took me from the ER
through two sets of seemingly airlocked double doors that
snapped shut like a trap behind me. The attendant asked me
a few questions, issued me my red scrubs, and confiscated my
belongings. As I changed in a guarded stall, I realized I'd finally
found the fine dining establishment sporks were designed for.

Welcome to Lockdown

I never planned to be there. I mean, who does? But one minute,
I was in the midst of my usual chaos, and the next, I had won
the golden ticket. Instead of leading to a tour of a magical
chocolate factory, it landed me under fluorescent lights,
gripping the armrests of a chair in what suspiciously felt like
a time-out corner for adults. The air felt heavy as my mind

capsized into anxiety. Waves of reality kept closing in: timed showers, no television to connect to news in the outside world, and ten-minute limits on phone calls with Philip.

In lockdown, I knew I was in for the long haul when they swapped my signature red medical scrubs that I was initially issued for street clothes—minus any potentially hazardous features like hooks or straps (naturally, for my safety).

I'd known for years that bras could be considered a deadly weapon, but this was the first time the medical establishment agreed with me.

I got sneaky by hiding in the corner of the phone table and extending my ten-minute calls with Philip as long as possible. Those two short daily calls were my only tether to the outside world. I couldn't shake the overwhelming guilt, questioning if I had done something so terrible to deserve this prison sentence. I thought I was just having a rough patch. A bad season. A moment. I tried to explain this to the psychiatrist, but apparently, a person explaining why they don't belong in a psych ward while turning four shades of red and wildly gesturing with their hands is not the most convincing argument. He didn't have to ponder too long about my condition; he was staring at a full-blown psychotic episode.

sticky note to self

Beneath our titles and roles, we're all humans navigating storms with limited capacities.

When my younger brother finally brought Philip, to visit a few days after my check-in, he spent the visit suppressing laughter, while my husband held back tears of his own private breakdown as I elaborated on the expansion of my grand company's sticky note puzzle.

That about summed up my state of mind. And yet, even in my delusions, I wasn't the only one struggling.

The ward was anything but silent. Random screams echoed from behind locked doors, the ones only staff could open. I told myself I was fine, that I didn't belong there. I just needed to return to my life—to work and normalcy. But the truth was, I wasn't doing great. Not even a little bit.

A Shaky Reality

The thing about being locked in with other unstable people is that you start realizing how fragile stability is. Breakdown doesn't care about your background, your status, or how many "strong friend" badges you've collected. I met people I once would've judged—people battling addiction, people with nowhere to go, people who had attempted to end their lives more times than they could count. And yet, here we were, eating with plastic utensils, bonding over group therapy games, and trying to keep our heads above water.

Here's the kicker: I grew up believing that the **best** way to deal with trauma was to bury it. We've all been programmed with the same old adage: "Out of sight, out of mind." If I ignored it long enough, maybe it would go away. I found myself watching the other patients. Some of them scared me—if I'd seen them on the street, I would've crossed to the other side. But then I was submerged in the ice bath of reality: Wait. Am I equally scary? Would someone look at me in my red scrubs, mumbling about sticky note empires, and run the other direction?

There was nowhere to go with that realization. No escape hatch. I was HERE—with THEM.

And I felt this weird compulsion to prove myself—like I needed everyone to know I had a respectable job, a family, a LIFE outside these walls. While others were slaying dragons and toting magic beans, I was clinging to my credentials like they still mattered. Like they made me different. Like they proved I didn't belong here. But the truth was staring me in the face: none of that mattered anymore. In here, we were all just the red team.

From Pencils of Yellow to Clothed in Red

I never imagined I'd end up sitting in red scrubs in a psych ward. But between the fluorescent lights and plastic utensils, here are some things that you need to know:

- **Your feelings aren't "just in your head."** They are IN your head, which is exactly where your entire nervous system gets its orders. So yeah, they're affecting everything. Don't let anyone minimize that.

- **Your treatment won't be like everyone else's.** Don't let them convince you to do what they're doing. What works for your sister's anxiety or your coworker's depression might do absolutely nothing for you. Speak up about what's working and what isn't—you're the one living in your brain, not your well-meaning friends with their "heard it on a podcast" recommendations.

- **Mental health isn't a "fix it once and forget it" situation.** It's more like having a temperamental car that needs regular check-ins even when it's running fine. Build in time to pause and process. It's not dramatic—it's maintenance.

- **A few good days don't mean you're cured.** Don't let a week of feeling stable convince you to fire your therapist and go rogue. That's like watching one YouTube video and deciding to do your own dental work. Just...don't.

The Faces I'd Rather Not See (That's My Face)

You know those people at street corners, the ones you pretend not to notice while waiting for the light to change? I was an expert at looking away. My brain had a whole filing system of judgments ready to deploy...

I don't feel safe with these people in my neighborhood.

They're choosing to live like this.

They probably aren't going to church.

They probably just got out of jail.

They're probably too lazy to work.

Why don't they just go to the local shelter?

How can they take care of that poor dog?

I stacked these judgments like armor, believing I would never live in their reality.

Then I found myself in red scrubs, watching my belongings disappear into a plastic bag.

That person mumbling to themselves on the bus? They might have the same diagnosis I do. That person seeking relief wherever they can find it? Maybe they're trying to silence the same screaming thoughts that my prescribed medications now quiet.

Here's what hit me: I had fail-safes a lot of people don't.

Short-term disability insurance. Health coverage that included psychiatric care. Medications I could actually afford. A support system waiting on the other side of those locked doors. Family who could visit. Friends who fed my dogs and drove my kids to school. Family Medical Leave Act protection so I had a job to return to. But what about the people who have none of that?

Now when I see someone struggling, my brain goes somewhere different...

That could be me without my medication.

That could be me without insurance.

That could be me if I couldn't afford treatment.

That could be me if I didn't have short-term disability.

Actually, that IS me—just with different resources.

Remember what I said about bones and dirt? We're all made of the same stuff. The only difference is some of us have better places to hide our mess.

The Best of Not Being In a Good Place

What would happen if we deflected our impulse to judge others? What if we shifted our thinking to assume that people are doing the best they can? This mindset would actually improve our lives. Through this realization, I came to understand that my goal should be to center my view of life around the desire for understanding—not necessarily to understand someone's specific situation, but to recognize that anyone is capable of anything. I realized that I needed to always lean into empathy. I also came to realize these truths:

In regards to anyone's mental health journey, we are all just trying to figure out which buttons not to push and how to make our lives easier to walk through.

Every person you pass has a story that would break your heart or light up your world—sometimes both.

The gap between 'them' and 'us' is about as wide as a safety net—one good support system makes all the difference.

Recovery isn't a straight line to "this brain is functioning as it should"—it's more like a game of Chutes and Ladders where everyone's board looks different.

When you stop seeing broken people and start seeing survivors, you might recognize the one in your mirror.

I think about my roommate in the ward, who had made multiple suicide attempts. She could have been any suburban mom at a PTA meeting. The only difference between me and the person sleeping on the street corner might be that I had somewhere to go and the resources I needed when the ward doors opened.

What if, instead of looking away, we looked closer? What if instead of judgment, we offered the grace we might need someday? Because here's the head crushing reality that I refused to "recover from" when I exited lockdown:

The line between "us" and "them" isn't just thin—it's imaginary.

The Beautiful Tearing of Pictures, Words, and Paste

Even in lockdown, my brain was still spinning at a million miles per hour. In one particular group therapy session, while others colored inside the lines, I lost myself in creating collages that reflected the beautiful ripped random pieces of my mind. We passed around magazines. I flipped through and tore out images of flowers, splashes of paint, and random words that sparkled with possibility. No scissors, of course—just ripping, arranging, and creating.

Each torn piece told a story: glossy petals from a perfume ad next to words like "dream" and "soar" ripped from motivational articles, paint swatches torn from home improvement features that bled into headlines about transformation. The collages became maps of my mind—disjointed yet somehow perfect, fragments of beauty emerging from chaos. Throughout that session, with cheap glue and determination, I created these visual manifestos of all I wanted to be, all I thought I could be, and all I was afraid I'd never be.

Later in a small group session, sitting eye to eye with other patients, I finally shared what brought me there—the pressure, the breaking point, the collapse. One of my fellow patients simply said, "I can understand how you were pushed. Don't feel bad about the things you did before you got here. You were in a dark place. Don't feel ashamed for ending up here. You are just where you need to be—consider it forced rest." In that moment, I felt seen.

We weren't just patients but artists in our own right, the 'red team' who happened to end up in the same dorm at summer camp, bound by our collective instability and the matching check-in scrubs.

Everyone had a story to tell...some of them hit home, some of them involved magic beans and a golden egg laying goose. I was mostly struck by how each of us expressed our inner worlds—through games of Apples to Apples and sharing crayons at the craft table.

Between the ripped-up pages and scribbled sticky note poetry, my thoughts found their way out—fragmented but fierce, shard-pieced mosaics. My "business meetings" consisted of explaining to anyone who would listen how my sticky note empire would revolutionize the world, while my poetry sprawled across tiny yellow squares told a different story. Each sticky note, whether filled with business schemes or poetry, became a piece of my scattered self finding its way back together.

Breaking Diamonds from the Dirt

As I sat cross-legged in the middle of the ward's hallway, scribbling a poem on a tiny sticky note, George, one of the night watch orderlies, approached and leaned casually against the wall across from me. He asked what I was writing. I told him I was a writer and editor for a Christian teen magazine, though at that moment, I wasn't sure I'd ever write anything respected in the professional world again. I told him what chaos had brought me to this place. Then I shared this poem I'd written across multiple sticky notes, words crammed into every available space:

> *in the soulful reflection beyond this place in time*
> *life is a means of souled dependence*
> *we all come crashing down to feel the reality*

> *there is only so much you can capably carry*
> *bones were not designed for weighty bags*
> *hands won't know that until they unknuckle*
> *fighting the untapped instinct to move to the next thing*
> *silencing voices that keep the mind turning 'round*
> *shaping comfort from chains that should never have been*
> *choosing once more the youth-filled folly*
> *that stabbed you in the back*
> *in the vulnerable turning—dry skin to a pillar of salt*
> *you have to steady before you can fly*
> *you have to scissor the tangled of minds*
> *In the relearn of normals and the move to glorious news*

I don't remember what George said. I don't even know if he said anything at all. But I remember the way he listened—really listened—to a manic woman sitting cross-legged on a sterile white floor that had its own share of dirt hiding in the cracks, reading poetry off sticky notes like they were sacred texts.

And maybe, just maybe they were.

Less Pride and Prejudice (But More Random Pieces of Paper)

Days blurred together in the ward. At some point, I brought my crumpled sticky note poem to group therapy, hoping to extract profound meaning from what felt like nonsense. What emerged, though, was an unexpected revelation: the wisdom gained from my time in the "slammer" ran deeper than I imagined. The prison wasn't just the physical ward—it was the mental fortress I'd constructed long before admission.

I had joined The Breakfast Club for the Unstable, only to discover something needed to be divinely drop-kicked out of me—pride. The questions haunted me:

Did I want to keep playing pretend?

Would I let pride hold me hostage?

Could I embrace authenticity, or would I lock those parts away once I left?

In the psych ward, I discovered more than just help—I found a voice for authentic advocacy. So go ahead, label me "unstable." I wear it proudly. Because if my life serves any purpose, it's sharing this truth without shame:

The face of mental illness? It looks a lot like me. We're all a beautiful mix of dirt and diamonds from our divinely-sculpted imprint—messy to the core yet sparkling with undeniable worth.

And that same reflection? It is lavishly loved. It is worthy of grace. It is capable of healing. It is full of purpose. And most definitely, it is never alone.

#shortyellowpencilRX—Your Daily Dose

Share your secret superhero identity—the one you slip into when adulting gets too real? Does she have a name? Special powers? An impressive catchphrase when paying bills? (Double bonus if you dare to leave her cape at home and show up as just regular, amazing you.)

PAGE TURNER

Nobody hands you a "Congratulations on Your Mental Breakdown" Hallmark card when you leave the psych ward. But after a week in lockdown, I emerged with something better: the realization that maybe this wasn't just a breakdown—it was a Bob Ross moment. A happy little accident waiting to become a happy little tree, but I need more writing space, so head to the next page.

RANDOM DOODLE SPACE

And Now for Something
Completely Different
(Understanding the Wiring)

Your Bit of Tooth Broccoli

is Full of Bonsai Potential

Chapter 5

From Head-In Collisions to

Happy Little Faceplants

(Painting the Scenery of New Perspective)

When my brain broke, it felt like the end. My life as a respected writer and a role model for kids, seemed irreparably shattered. Suddenly, driving a car felt like navigating a spaceship through an asteroid field. Cooking dinner became the equivalent of solving an advanced calculus problem—I was missing half the numbers, and the teacher just walked out of the room.

Even the simplest things felt monumental. I'd find myself touching the back of my head, to check that my brain wasn't exposed—because that's how it felt. My family handled everything from grocery shopping to ensuring I didn't wander off mid-sentence like some confused side character in a sitcom.

And then came the shame. Oh, the shame.

The Uninvited Houseguest

Shame didn't just visit; it moved in, unpacked its bags, and started redecorating. It whispered things like, "You're broken. You'll never recover. People will never respect you after this."

Then it added the most painful whisper of all: "If they knew your whole story, they would never stick around, let alone trust anything you have to say again."

Shame isn't subtle—it's like that one overzealous aunt at Thanksgiving who points out all your flaws, suggests a new diet plan, and then asks if you've thought about doing something with your hair. Except this one doesn't go home when the pie is gone.

But shame doesn't stop at making you feel inadequate. It convinces you that your struggle is a moral failure.

That somehow, my inability to "snap out of it" meant I was defective—or worse, a spiritual disappointment. Shame loves to tell you that your mess disqualifies you from being used by God, as if He only works with people who have pristine résumés and zero baggage.

Barefaced in the Church Balcony (some more God stuff)
Church is supposed to be a sanctuary where we can be real, right? A place where we can be honest with God without the performance—without the makeup. But let's face it—being honest with His followers? That's where it gets tricky.

sticky note to self

Faith never requires the denial of harsh realities.

Some Sundays, I'd sit in my car in the church parking lot, staring at the doors like they were the gates to a very polite inquisition. That's why I started sneaking into the empty balcony on Wednesday nights— just to listen to the worship team practice in the dark. No expectations, no plastered smiles—just me, the music, the glow of my laptop for my random thoughts, and the unmistakable smell of hymnals.

It's hard to walk into a room full of smiling faces, knowing the mask of expectations is keeping the sides of your lips pulled up. It's even harder when you sense that the people around you are just as broken, but too afraid to admit it.

It wasn't that I lacked grace for people—I just didn't have the energy for conversations. I didn't need another round of unsolicited spiritual advice or someone telling me to "just trust God more." That advice was right up there with telling someone who can't sleep to just "relax." (By the way, my version of relaxing included Ambien-induced sleepwalking, only to wake up under a pile of chocolate wrappers the next day.)

What I needed wasn't more advice or platitudes. What I needed was space to be real with God—no interruptions, no performance, just raw honesty in that quiet balcony.

Happy Little Accident Theology

Like many people who've hit rock bottom, I found healing in unexpected places. For me, it started with Bob Ross and ended in deeper faith, but the journey there wasn't what anyone would have predicted.

I grew up watching "The Joy of Painting," and Bob's voice was the emotional support blanket I didn't know I needed. Unsurprisingly, he retired from a life of perfectly lined-up, military-induced stress to creating forests of happy little trees, teaching us all not to panic when a brushstroke went awry. He didn't throw the canvas out or start over. Instead, he'd smile and say, "We don't make mistakes; we make happy little accidents." Then, with a few flicks of his brush, he'd turn that accident into a happy little tree.

It was a revelation: mistakes weren't something to hide. They were opportunities in disguise—sometimes messy, sometimes hilarious, but opportunities nonetheless.

When we stop trying to keep up appearances, we create space for real hurt, real connection, real healing and, where my "happy little accidents" thrive, real humor.

Taking my cue from Bob, I realized the very things I wanted to hide—the rabid baboon graffiti in my story—could become the bridge that would be divinely repurposed to connect with others. Not through polished perfection, but through honest faceplants. (And let's be real, faceplants are the only kind of plants I know I can grow, unless you count the fake ones in my garden.)

Speaking of things that grow, my tooth gap has a special talent for catching spinach. Some people spot that leafy green decoration and tell everyone but me (because public humiliation is their spiritual gift). But the real ones? They'll catch my eye, grin, and say "You saving that for later?" And even after I tell them I'm storing it up for winter, they still want to do lunch again—because they know these little moments are just part of my charm.

Whether you find your peace in a church balcony or somewhere else entirely, the key is finding that quiet space where you can be completely honest about your struggles. For me, that meant pulling God's face in close when everything else felt far away.

Survival Wasn't Glamorous

It didn't look like a phoenix rising from the ashes. No, it looked like me trying to cook spaghetti while forgetting to boil the water. It looked like struggling to remember the way to the grocery store I'd been to a hundred times— then having an existential crisis in the peanut butter aisle before retreating to my car to assume the fetal position.

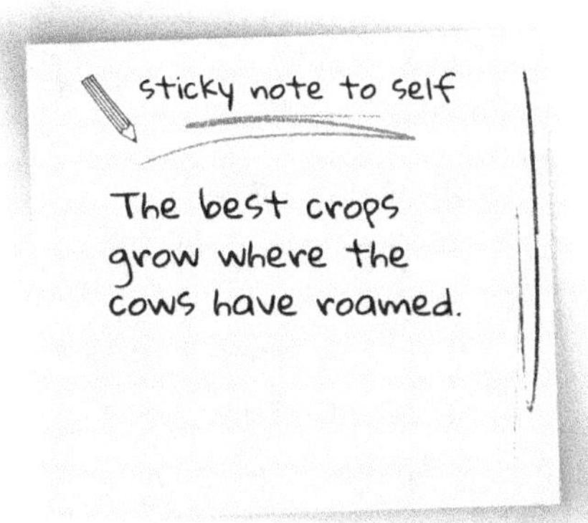

Here's what I learned: Hobbling is healing. Resting isn't failing— it's necessary. Accepting help is wisdom, not weakness. And recovery isn't about independence; it's about connection.

The journey forward requires both hands—yours and others'.

How to Not Drown Your Lifeguards

If I wanted grace, I had to extend it to the people caring for me, too. My family was walking this journey with me, and I had to learn to tell them what I actually needed instead of expecting them to read my mind. Shocking, I know. I recognized their efforts, even when imperfect. I showed appreciation. And I found ways to take small steps on my own so they could breathe, too. Every small step I took helped me build muscle for bigger issues—and kept me from drowning the people trying to help me.

The Ministry of Happy Little Faceplants

Here's the thing about faceplants: they're universally humbling. There's nothing quite like realizing you've been walking around with spinach in your teeth to remind you that you're gloriously human.

At first, I treated my faceplants like evidence that I was failing. I wanted to be that polished leader, the one with all the answers tucked neatly in her back pocket. Instead, I became the person everyone politely avoided eye contact with because I was clearly "going through something."

And then came the job interviews. I thought being honest about my mental health journey would be a point of connection—turns out, it's not exactly the bullet point hiring managers are looking for. I nailed questions about my skills and accolades (years of award-winning magazine experience, mind you), but the moment I mentioned my desire to write and speak openly about mental health, the air got thinner. Smiles tightened. Pens stopped scribbling.

One particular online interview wrapped up so fast, I wouldn't have been surprised if they hit "Force Quit" on the meeting as soon as I said goodbye.

After that? Radio silence. No calls, no emails, not even a courtesy rejection letter.

Here's what I couldn't shake: every time I was honest about my mental health—the real, daily struggle, not the polished testimony—doors closed. All my experience meant nothing once 'ongoing mental health issues' entered the chat. They weren't being cruel. They were being careful. But I needed somewhere my mess was useful, not disqualifying. This wasn't that place.

However I didn't want to spend my energy fuming because I didn't get the job I thought I deserved. I quickly realized these faceplants—maybe they weren't disasters, but doorways? Not just for me, but for others who needed to know they weren't alone in their struggles. And then I remembered Bob Ross and his happy little accidents. Each "mistake" on his canvas became the foundation for something unexpected and beautiful. Maybe these faceplants weren't deviations from my ministry—maybe they WERE my ministry.

Some of my best connections have come from my messiest moments. Vulnerability has a way of breaking downwalls that perfectionism built.

I used to think healing was about fixing everything that felt broken. But now I know healing is more about learning to move forward even when things still feel a little wobbly. My brain still tries to outrun itself. Some days, my emotions want to stage a full-blown coup—if I can even remember what I'm supposed to be doing. And honestly? I get so freaking tired trying to hog-tie them all down, and that's with my meds.

The real work? Learning to live, breathe, and keep going through it—not waiting until everything is neat, tidy, and presentable. Because if I waited for that, I'd never get anywhere.

And that's the real takeaway: you don't have to be symptom-free to succeed in life. You don't have to have everything figured out to take the next step. You just have to decide you're going to keep showing up. Besides, every great comeback story starts with a "Well, that didn't go as planned" moment.

#shortyellowpencilRX—Your Daily Dose

Think of a time you faceplanted (literally or figuratively) and somehow it worked out. What hilarious or helpful lesson did you learn? Bonus points if you also get actual plants stuck in your teeth—this means we're definitely related.

PAGE TURNER

This journey isn't just my story—it's also the story of those who catch us when we fall. Like my British husband, who had to trade his stiff upper lip for a softer approach to life. What does "in sickness and in health" really look like when your wife's brain is constantly recalculating? Philip answers next—in the Queen's English, naturally. (You'll see "colour" and "favour" spelled properly for a change.)

This is an Ex-Parrot

(nailing reality to the perch of life)

Take Time to Wave Back

to the Flowers & Sausages
on Your Path

Chapter 6

'Ello from the Other Side:
(A Brit's Guide to Loving a Whirlwind Wife)

I didn't marry a damsel in distress. I married a force of nature—a free spirit, intelligent, and utterly relentless in her passion. Amber could outtalk a room of barristers and break into British comedy sketches with impeccably witty timing alongside me.

Let me be crystal clear—I didn't sign up for a quiet life. But I did like structure and a predictable routine from day-to-day. When I met Amber, I knew I was embarking on an adventure that made my pre-Amber life resemble a particularly dull episode of *Antiques Roadshow*.

Our story began, as many do, with Amber's college roommate who introduced us as pen pals, which soon turned into a series of spectacularly miscalculated long-distance communications. Imagine, if you will, a bright-eyed American girl who rings me up on my birthday in October of 1993 at two in the morning London time, completely oblivious to the exact time difference. Instead of being annoyed, we ended up quoting *Monty Python* for an hour, most assuredly disturbing all those who were trying to sleep. Sensible people would have written this call off as a wrong number. Not us.

That's when I knew—this woman, brave enough to ring a man, practically a stranger, in the middle of the night for his birthday, and witty enough to warrant a night of lost sleep—was something special. By mid-December, what started as friendly calls had blossomed into romance. This was indeed divinely orchestrated providence. What really stole her heart? When she fell ill during winter break, I sent her my childhood teddy bear and a massive Cadbury milk chocolate bar, amongst other souvenirs and photographs—a proper care package from across the pond. It might have seemed silly to some, sending a grown woman a teddy bear, but sometimes comfort comes in the most unexpected forms.

Our methods of communication were hardly conventional. Letters that crossed continents, phone calls that cost more than the average rent of a luxury flat, and a shared love language of British comedy that could bridge any geographical divide. We exchanged mix tapes filled with songs that spoke what our hearts couldn't quite say across the distance.

The Pedestal Problem

My first blunder in marriage? Building pedestals. Like an overeager architect with more ambition than sense, I constructed one so towering for Amber that when reality came barging in, the whole thing came crashing down with all the grace of a toddler discovering gravity. Quite the spectacle, really.

Even before we tied the knot, I'd scripted the scene straight out of a Jane Austen novel in my head. In May, Amber was to arrive for a three-month holiday at my parents' home, and, as an Anglophile, I'd imagined her spellbound by the landscape. Instead, my American dream girl dozed off shortly after we pulled out of Victoria Station, leaving a rather impressive puddle of drool on my shoulder. At least she was comfortable.

As it turns out, romance has a rather clever way of dismantling one's carefully constructed illusions of perfection.

I hadn't anticipated how this beautiful cyclone would thoroughly test my patience, resilience, and understanding of what being a husband meant—especially when, three months later, we, rather spontaneously and without reserve, decided to elope before she was to return for her final year at college. This also made her spontaneously postpone her return to the States for another year and a half, 'til I could join her. My parents were round the corner doing the shopping whilst we were at the local Registry Office with a couple of my friends, but then nothing about us has ever been particularly by the book.

A Brit Abroad Without His Bearings

After a year and a half as honeymooners living in my childhood home in north London with my parents, we decided to move to the States so Amber could finish her final year of college. Moving to Springfield, Missouri—smack in the centre of America—was my first real lesson in humility.

Here I was, a proud Brit, suddenly rendered completely helpless in the heart of the American Midwest. I'd never ventured further west than Florida before this leap of faith. No reliable public transport. No ability to drive due to my limited eyesight. Absolute dependency on Amber for basic errands. Nothing quite strips away a man's ego like having to ask his wife for a ride to the local shops.

Beyond that, everything seemed backwards. Light switches turned the opposite way. Hot and cold water taps were reversed. I had to watch that I wouldn't be taken out at a road crossing because everyone here drives on the wrong side of the road. And the number of times I ordered a Diet Coke only to receive a Dr. Pepper seemed comically absurd. One of my fellow ex-pats was told by a pharmacist that she had a speech impediment. She had to explain, "No, I'm English."

But we adapted. We always do. 

Where I brought structure, Amber brought the spark of chaotic brilliance. Where she'd start seventeen projects, I'd take things off her plate (a majority of which involved ordering a takeaway for supper).

Because of the number of times she'd lose her keys, I'd developed an uncanny ability to locate them in completely illogical places, even with my vision impairment. But even adorable quirks come with weighty realities.

Long Distance Dreams & One-On-One Realities

Marriage, I presumed, would be about shared laughter over breakfast, long walks at the park, and the occasional squabble over whose turn it was to do the washing up. We weren't terribly civilised—more like one step away from embracing the life of college students living on ramen noodles and laundry that went from one dishevelled clean pile to a somewhat soiled pile, still equally adequate for one more day of wear. But no one pulls you aside when you're exchanging vows to mention those moments when the person you cherish starts unravelling before your eyes.

In fact, I was oblivious to any significant mental health red flags for the first nineteen years of our marriage, because our minds were so preoccupied with life—Amber finishing school, getting jobs to pay the bills, and then six years later having our first kid that eventually increased to three.

For six months, I watched Amber write obsessively—pages and pages, day and night, barely sleeping. The words poured out faster than she could capture them. I knew something was wrong, but I didn't know what to do about it.

A cuppa won't fix everything, but it gives you a moment to figure out what might.

Naturally, I initially fell back on what any proper British husband would do—maintain composure, establish order, focus on the practical. Ensure the kids were fed, dressed, and ready for school. Put the kettle on, because surely a nice cuppa fixes everything. Mental health, as it turns out, has absolutely no respect for logic, and even Twinings' finest blend can't calm a storm once it's in full swing.

So began my education—a painful one, if I'm honest. I discovered that Amber didn't need me to ride in and valiantly save the day. She needed me to be there, sitting in the eye of the hurricane with her, holding her hand when words felt as useless as wearing wellies in a swimming pool. She needed to know that she wasn't facing it alone, even when everything else had toppled.

But that's barely scratching the surface of our story.

A Rather Time Lord-ish Adventure: Navigating the Wibbly-Wobbly World of Mental Health

It was during one particularly memorable therapy session that the counsellor delivered what I now consider the understatement of the decade: "You know you will always be married to a bipolar woman, right?" That was rather like being smacked round the head with a cricket bat. I'd treated each episode as a temporary inconvenience, like a bit of unfortunate weather that would eventually clear up. This revelation came after the proper wake-up call—the one that landed Amber in the psychiatric ward. But somehow, in my infinite wisdom, I'd convinced myself that I could prevent it from happening again with enough care and attention.

Let's just say missing even a day of medication can trigger anxiety-ridden mood swings that take weeks to stabilise, hence the daily check-off list I now maintain for her with religious devotion.

Mental health isn't a battle to be won, but rather a landscape to be navigated—think less military campaign, more an endless episode of DOCTOR WHO where you're never quite sure what you'll discover once the TARDIS doors open.

And what's going on in your brain, no matter how small, is always bigger on the inside. With Amber's bipolar disorder, some days are brilliant sunlit peaks; others are foggy valleys of inattentiveness and forgetfulness where even the simplest communication feels like trying to row a boat through porridge.

The British Caregiver's Guide to Keep Calm and Actually Carry On

Right then, here's what I've learnt about being the steady hand on the tiller of day-to-day life. And for what it's worth, what works for me is having the ability to reevaluate what "working" looks like. This comes with an earnest desire for heavenly insight (prayer—and lots of it), because sometimes only God knows the way forward (and He has yet to share His complete roadmap with me). But whilst waiting on divine direction, I've gathered a few earthly strategies that help keep our ship steady.

Partner, Not Therapist—Love doesn't cure mental illness any more than a cup of tea cures a broken leg. (Though the tea certainly doesn't hurt.) Your role isn't to fix—it's to create a hedgerow of safety whilst ensuring professional help remains part of the journey. Think of yourself as a dance partner rather than the choreographer—two entirely different jobs, both essential to the performance.

The Art of Steady Support— When Amber's mind feels like it's hosting a rock concert at Wembley Arena, she needs an anchor, not a hero. This means maintaining predictable routines whilst knowing when to step back. Some days require gentle consistency—regular schedules, calm responses, quiet encouragement. Other days call for strategic retreat—brewing that cuppa and waiting in the wings until she's ready. The trick is learning to read which is needed when.

Mind Your Mental Garden—Caregiver burnout is as fun as a wet holiday at the British seaside. Take care of yourself, or you'll be about as useful as a chocolate teapot. And don't be afraid to enlist the help of another support person you and your spouse both trust when you're exhausted.

Deploy Humour Strategically—Some days, the best medicine is a perfectly timed Monty Python reference or an absolutely rubbish dad joke. When all else fails, making her laugh at how spectacularly bad my joke was is always a good idea.

The real trick is maintaining perspective. Your partner isn't their diagnosis any more than my wife is her sometimes questionable taste in jumpers. They're whole, complex human beings navigating a rather challenging neurological landscape. Your job is to be the human equivalent of a satellite navigation system—constantly recalculating routes whilst maintaining a suspiciously calm voice about it all.

Marriage in these circumstances is rather like trying to waltz in clown shoes—it requires flexibility, dedication, and an absolutely unflagging sense of humour, knowing you are going to step on each other's toes. Some days, you'll be spot on with coordination; others, you'll both end up stepping all over each other. The key is no matter how much you get tripped up, you're committed to having another go. We've learnt to play to each other's strengths.

Where I bring methodical thinking, Amber brings get-it-done impulsivity—basically, she's the human equivalent of a verb.

I help her think through the possible impediments; she helps me see beyond the rigid boundaries. It's not about wishing the other person would change to be more like you but appreciating how various contrasts complement each other.

sticky note to self

Marriage is like a proper cup of PG Tips—good leaves, a raging boil, adequate timing, and the wrap of a knitted cosy.

And yes, sometimes you can only put the kettle on and take it one moment at a time. Because at the end of the day, love isn't about fixing—it's about being present, observant and focused on grace.

Remember, fellow caregivers: you're doing brilliantly, even when it feels like you're barely keeping your head above water.

Confessions of a Reformed Stiff Upper Lip

Here's a revelation that might have made my proper Englishman of a father raise an eyebrow: vulnerability is not failure. On the contrary, it is the secret sauce which transforms a marriage from a functional arrangement to a true partnership.

I've had to unlearn generations of British emotional restraint. No more stiff upper lip and stern looks to pre-empt potential embarrassment. Instead, honest conversations. Admitting when I'm overwhelmed, including the ability to shed a tear.

Finding Silver Linings in Rather Grey Skies

People often see mental health challenges as pure struggle. But there are unexpected gifts. Amber's condition has taught me a depth of compassion I never knew I possessed—but that did take years to develop. And mind you, the road was not lined with flowers and sausages for either of us. I had my share of overcoming my own dysfunction tasked to accomplish before I was capable of moving in a better direction. That didn't start until we both decided it was time for professional counselling, of which I highly recommend.

Getting this kind of assistance, though some men are diametrically opposed, is not weakness; it's showing great strength like the bravery of a knight to his lady to say: "You're of such great worth to my life, I'm willing to fight for you—to fight for us."

That takes a man of true courage.

This journey has shown me that love isn't about perfection but about choosing each other every single day.

Our home is far from a showroom of domestic harmony. It's a Picasso of half-finished projects, spontaneous dance parties, blackened meals, and moments of profound connection. Some days, success looks far from "Keep Calm and Carry On" and more like just dragging through the day.

A Nice Cuppa Love and Understanding

Marriage isn't about managing a condition. It's about creating a partnership where both individuals can thrive. Challenges are addressed, but don't define us. Love is not only about action, but sometimes inaction—corporately agreeing the only answer is to be still as only God can provide the answers. In both—it is an active, daily choice.

And if all else fails? There's always a Cadbury's Fruit and Nut Bar within a five-mile radius. It's her favourite. Thankfully available in America now, so I keep her prescription well-stocked. I've learnt to appreciate the whirlwind—we live in tornado alley, so I suppose it's fitting I married one. I wouldn't have it any other way.

#shortyellowpencilRX—Your Daily Dose

What are some of the small things that people do that put a smile on your face, or simply make you feel better? Extra points if it involves chocolate or random memes.

PAGE TURNER 

Speaking of tea, I've learnt to keep a watchful eye on the kettle—unlike my beloved wife, who has turned forgetting she put it on, only to return and find it tepid, into an Olympic sport. But that's just one of the many quirks that make our life together an adventure. I'll let her tell you about the spice her ADHD brings to our daily lives, starting with her legendary culinary experiments. (For me, the most memorable being her curried omelets.)

The Squirrels in Your Brain

Deserve a Coffee Break

Chapter 7

Help, I'm ADHD Adulting!
(From Willy Wonka'd Mealtimes to Pure Imagination)

Hey, it's Amber again. I'd like to formally thank my hubby for author bombing my book. So consider this the fast-forward moment — like Augustus Gloop being vacuum-transported from the chocolate river of suspense-filled psychosis (medically stabilized, by God's grace) straight into the boiler room messy of daily life.

During his takeover, I not only finished scribbling through sentences of this chapter discussing my superpower of ADHD, I manufactured another kitchen disaster. My daughter Pen said, "Mum, I know you have that chapter written, but I think this deserves a mention and perhaps a picture that says 'Exhibit A.'"

Well, I should have known that when I was hyper-focusing on writing a chapter about my ADHD, I would accidentally cook one of my good steak knives with a side of tots. If you need the recipe—just put one on a cookie sheet, 425 degrees for twenty minutes. You see, I'm the kind of chef who throws random ingredients together (including ingredients of the plastic variety) and then promptly forgets about it until the smoke alarm rouses me. Chef ADHD strikes again! Who knows, maybe that's how someone invented that "wax lip" candy. So, with this set up, I want to give you a Golden Ticket tour of my

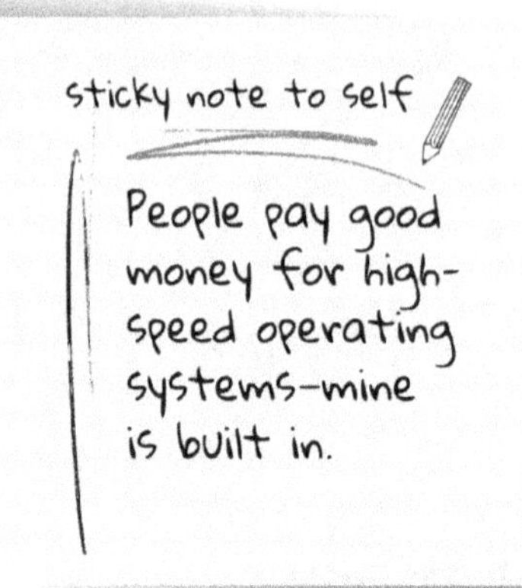

kitchen, where you might catch me staring at a battlefield of precooked frozen chicken, instant mashed potatoes (pro tip: xanthan gum is NOT a fix for thin potatoes), and whatever microwave-in-bag frozen vegetable I excavate from the bottom of the deep freeze. The walking-away-from-what's-cooking part isn't so good, but I like to combine some of these base time-saving ingredients with creative experimentation, because sometimes the most delicious discoveries come from minds that don't follow recipes.

Oompa Loompa, My Brain is Goopity Goo'd

It's Willy Wonka Sunday dinner time—the Gene Wilder version where he stirs the contents of a big copper candy cauldron, tastes it, and then casually drops an old boot in the pot. Tonight's culinary adventure features frozen yeast rolls that look like they've been half-raised from the dead. I poke them a bit—who would've guessed they'd spring a leak? No worries, butter fixes everything, right?

For the chicken, I grab whatever condiment catches my eye first. Oh wait—I wanted sweet chili sauce. Maybe if I mix chili powder with sweet and sour sauce? Close enough, right? Only after dumping it on do I realize it tastes nothing like what I imagined, but it's sparked an idea for a whole new sauce that might just work better. If it's edible, I count it as a win, and if it's surprisingly good, I credit my ADHD brain's knack for unexpected combinations. Sometimes these happy accidents turn into family favorites. And if we don't like it, at least the dogs will eat well that night—although they've criticized my cooking, too.

My brain works in bursts between 'squirrels on crack' and 'These squirrels are dead—bring in back-ups.' During hyper-focus, I'll lose myself perfecting a book cover design, only to snap back to reality when dark clouds billow from the oven—I swear that timer was silent for the past two minutes.

Somehow, we end up eating dinner at 9 p.m., the forgotten dishes still lounging in a sink of cold, sudsless water like abandoned pool floats.

Yes, these quirks come with their fair share of challenges, but they're also the spark behind every creative solution and improvised meal that turned out surprisingly amazing. Who has time to find measuring spoons when inspiration strikes? That looks 'about right' is my signature measurement style. Sure, sometimes our meals are blackened, and yes, occasionally a ceramic dish has exploded (my non-stick baking pans are definitely sticking these days). But even if it's not Pinterest-perfect, it's Facebook meme-worthy and Instagram story gold. These moments don't just make life interesting—they make it extraordinary, one burnt roll and accidental sauce discovery at a time.

When ADHD is Your Sous Chef of Life

This naturally-caffeinated brain setting is my secret weapon in the professional world. When I'm planning an issue of my magazine, *Leading Hearts*, planning a podcast or doing a graphic design project my hyperfocus becomes a superpower. Time fades away as creative work emerges, work that my clients applaud me for. Of course, I've developed little adaptations to help me process tasks better. Sometimes I listen with my eyes pointed down—or even closed. Blocking out competing external stimuli helps me "hear" better, as if turning down the visual noise lets my brain tune into the sound.

My creative chaos has a method to its madness. When a challenge pops up, my brain feels compelled to address it, even if it's not where I started. That magazine deadline? I'll stay on target until it's done and done well. But in this creative zone, time turns into a black hole—bathroom breaks become optional, I forget to pick up Pen at school, and dinner becomes a concept rather than a reality. I've learned to adjust to these natural rhythms, creating systems that work with my mind rather than against it. The traits that make me an adventurous cook are the same ones that fuel my success as a creative professional. That ability to improvise a sauce from random ingredients? It's the same skill that helps me piece together book covers from 20 layers of scattered elements.

When a project needs a fresh perspective, my mind is ready to roll with an insight that demands experimentation.

In life, as in cooking, every task becomes an opportunity for innovation. Sometimes that means discovering brilliant solutions through unexpected paths, sometimes it means adapting on the fly. But whether I'm using scissors to ninja-blade my steak or ironing with a wet washcloth and dryer sheet (actual irons are fire hazards—I've melted clothes), my brain is ready to troubleshoot—even if the process looks more like a smoke-filled cooking show than a controlled lab experiment.

I Love Lucy Meets Adobe Creative Suite: A Multitasking Adventure

You know that iconic *I Love Lucy* scene where Lucy and Ethel are working in the chocolate factory? They're overwhelmed, frantic, and chaos ensues as the chocolates pile up faster than they can handle on the conveyor belt. That's what it feels like when I'm deep in creative work—except instead of chocolates, it's deadlines, designs, and decisions coming at me all at once. Just like Lucy and Ethel found creative ways to handle those chocolates (even if their solutions weren't exactly factory-approved), I've developed my own tactics like mixing Photoshop's powerful design capabilities with Canva's user-friendly platform, creating campaign templates that work smarter, not harder. Better yet, I teach my clients these hacks too—because everyone deserves to know how to catch their chocolates before they hit the floor. Turns out, this creative problem-solving runs in the family. My dad, a typesetter, hacked his system to accomplish the equivalent of desktop publishing before it even existed. Some might call it disorder, but I call it innovative thinking passed down through the gene pool.

sticky note to self

I am actively perfecting the fine art of randomness.

Like Lucy, however, I can hyper-focus on one thing while everything else piles up in the background. My living space may end up looking like a college dorm during finals week—creative chaos in its natural habitat. But you know what? I've learned to embrace it. Each project I tackle is like scaling a mountain, and when I reach that summit-pure adrenaline rush. The dishes might be staging a rebellion in the sink, but hey—at least my client loved their book cover.

My workspace adapts like Lucy's chocolate-hiding spots—not confined to a desk, because creative inspiration doesn't wait for the perfect setting. Those fifteen minutes in the car waiting for the person I need to pick up? That's prime article-writing time with my laptop setup. (Side note: My husband found a little laptop desk attachment for my steering wheel. Brilliant invention, but you can't drive with it—I'd say it's the world's best reminder to stay focused while operating a motor vehicle.)

Like Lucy and Ethel facing judgment (and probably a pink slip) at that chocolate factory, my unconventional work style comes with its critics, more often than not, the loudest one is in my own head.

Everyone's a Critic (Especially Me)

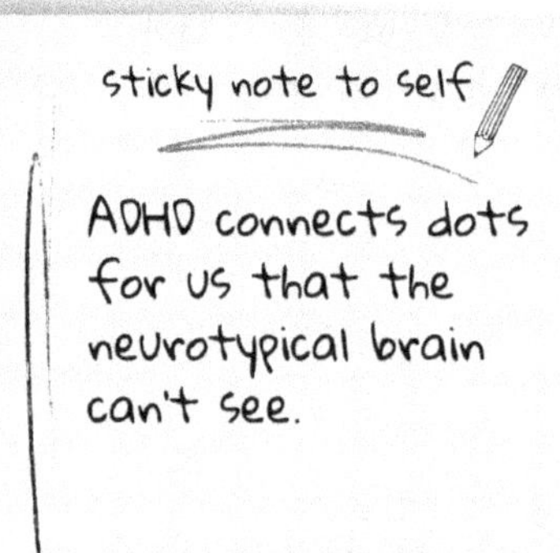

Sometimes the hardest part isn't the ADHD itself—it's the running commentary in our heads, that mashup of inner critic and everyone else's voice. We're masters at absorbing other people's judgments and turning them into *Self-Doubts— The Greatest Hits* album.

When someone walks in and sees me staring blankly into space, dirty dishes piled in the sink, their judgment is practically radiating: another mess, another task left undone. My inner voice chimes in on cue: "Why can't you just be normal and keep up with basic cleaning?" What they don't see is that my brain is simultaneously mapping three client projects, tracking my daughter's assignments (because ADHD runs in the family), and calculating how many fifteen-minute chunks fit between Zoom calls before the dishes become a science experiment.

The "you're so disorganized" comments hit particularly hard, especially when my inner voice adds its own special remix: "They're right—look at this chaos. A real adult would have this figured out by now." But here's what they're missing:

my brain isn't disorganized—it's hyper-organized in its own unique language. Like those paintings that turn into an entirely different picture when you step back and refocus. Those can look like chaos within an intricate system of perfectly sensible connections—and honestly it makes me a bit dizzy sometimes but I love it. Those scattered sticky notes across the bedside table? They're arranged by project urgency, even if nobody else can decode the system.

The worst accusation, though, is when people assume I'm "just being lazy." That one sneaks past my defenses and whispers: "What if they're right? What if I'm just making excuses?"

But that pile of laundry they're judging? It represents active prioritization, not laziness. I've calculated the return on investment of putting away clothes versus finishing a client deadline, factored in who needs clean underwear most urgently, and decided my creative energy is better spent elsewhere right now. It's not perfect, but it's strategic chaos.

When ADHD Is Your Superpower

Let's talk superpowers—and I don't mean the kind that involves radioactive spiders and spandex (although I do love the "sucking in" power of Spanx). These supposedly scattered brains come with their own special set of abilities that, when understood and embraced, become secret weapons.

The 'Time Isn't Real' Superpower—Start working at 2 p.m. and suddenly it's midnight, with no memory of eating, drinking, or acknowledging the outside world? That's hyperfocus, baby! While everyone else portions their day into responsible little chunks, we're out here bending the space-time continuum to crush entire projects in what feels like minutes. (Just maybe set a timer to remind you that food and bathroom breaks are still a thing.)

The 'Connect ALL The Dots!' Power—Picture a conspiracy theory board, but for actually useful stuff. While others draw nice, straight lines between related ideas, we're playing mental Twister, connecting that random penguin fact from third grade to our current work project. And somehow? It actually works. After years of forcing my square-peg brain into round-hole productivity strategies, I've learned to embrace this unique operating system by creating an environment that works with my mind, not against it.

The 'Chaos to Clarity' Conversion—Have you ever been in a meeting and everyone's staring at a problem, completely stuck, and your brain goes "Oh! What if we tried this completely bonkers thing that might work?"' That's the superpower of mining mental chaos to find creative gold. Sometimes it leads to 3:00 a.m. inspiration to put together a design experiment on my phone. Because when I have a thought, I have to capture it immediately or it vanishes like smoke.

The 'Productive Procrastination' Paradox—When avoiding one task, we become unstoppable at everything else. Need to write a report? Suddenly you're sorting through the sock drawer to remove all the ones with holes while simultaneously solving world hunger. The trick is harnessing this power—sometimes the best way to get something done is to pretend you're supposed to be doing something else.

The 'Brain-Saving Automation' System
The 'Decision Fatigue Defense '— Minimize your wardrobe like a cartoon character with a closet full of the same outfit. It's not boring, it's brilliant. When your brain's running a million background processes, choosing between forty-seven slightly different black shirts isn't how you want to start your day. Pro

tip: Buy identical socks for everyone in the house—instant mate-matching magic.

The 'Future Me Thanks Past Me' Protocol—If you use the last of something, tell Siri to add it to your shopping list like you're leaving messages in a time capsule. Future you will be amazed at past you's responsibility (and probably suspicious about what else you're up to).

The 'Food Management Made Simple' Solution—Make meals automatic. Monday means pasta, Tuesday brings tacos—your week runs on a dependable food schedule. Stock an Emergency Food Kit with zero-brain-power frozen meals for those days when cooking isn't happening. Create a 'Can't Fail' grocery essentials list with ingredients that make at least three different meals when inspiration runs dry.

On that note, instead of taking you further into information overload paralysis, I have a gift for you: I've compiled ten practical ADHD survival strategies—everything from managing decision fatigue to never losing your keys again. But listing them all here would make this chapter longer than an ADHD person can handle in one sitting. So I've put them in a free downloadable toolkit at *www.shortyellowpencilrx.com/ADHDToolkit*. Print it, bookmark it, screenshot it—whatever works for your brain. Trust me, you'll want to reference these when you need them, not right now when you're in the middle of all these words.

Your Best is The Best (Even When Your Brain Screams It's Not Enough)

'Doing your best' doesn't mean getting everything right or matching everyone else's Pinterest-perfect version of success. Some days, ADHD feels like being trapped in a hamster wheel of "should"—should do more, should work harder, should have finished that yesterday.

Breaking free from that cycle feels wrong, like I'm giving up or letting someone down.

But here's the truth: self-advocacy becomes revolutionary because until we speak up, others don't know our struggles or what helps us succeed. They don't see the mental tug-of-war behind every "simple" task.

Sometimes, my best means simply getting through the day without drowning in the guilt of a forgotten task (or three… or five). Sometimes, it's showing up at 40 percent capacity and remembering that I wasn't designed to carry everything alone. For me, that means trusting that God multiplies everything I don't have the strength to accomplish—He wants me to rely on Him when my executive function decides to take an unscheduled vacation. Your support system might look different, and that's okay. But the end goal is the epiphany moment: realizing we weren't built to do this alone.

And if we're lowering the bar for ourselves, we must be willing to do the same for others. Because ADHD makes us impatient with "how slow" people respond to our needs—if you haven't noticed that yet. Grace, humor, and patience become your secret weapons, both for yourself and those around you.

And when dinner is burnt again? There's always takeout. My van's GPS has already mapped my favorite rescue locations.

sticky note to self

My inbox reached epic status. So I marked everything as read and called it a filing system.

Sometimes the best solution is knowing when to call in reinforcements—and when to order DoorDash.

#shortyellowpencilRX—Your Daily Dose

What are the important tasks you hilariously (or embarrassingly) neglect? Cleaning the bathroom? Buying groceries? What do you have to do to get those things accomplished (or do you)? Subtract points if you, like me, have to clean angry.

PAGE TURNER

You know what really hates chaos? The control I think I can wrangle in from my collection of big BUTs—those things we do in the name of control that actually keep us stuck. "But I have to do it perfectly." "But what if I fail?" "But people will judge me." These BUTs aren't protecting us; they're paralyzing us. And I'm not just talking about the physical one that made me embrace my capsule wardrobe of one-size-fits-all black yoga pants (remember that decision fatigue defense?).

Now, make sure you break out of that focus trance and check the time (or at least go to the bathroom) before heading to the next chapter with me. Because we're about to talk about how those BUTs and other control mechanisms keep us from the freedom we're actually craving.

RANDOM DOODLE SPACE

RANDOM DOODLE SPACE

Need More Nuts in Your Life?

Become an Elephant Tamer

Chapter 8

I Have a Big BUT Problem
(The Tale of Four Big Buts)

Let's start with an admission: I have a big plus-sized butt. And it has a nasty habit of getting in the way. It's the kind that makes buying jeans a full-contact sport and sitting in plastic chairs a game of architectural trust. But let's not get hung up on that particular big butt (though I am always trying to downsize it). Today, we're talking about my other big BUT problem—the one that rears its stubborn head whenever I face a challenge I can't immediately solve.

Here's how it works: A problem arises. Instead of addressing it outright, I hush it up, retreat to my mental workshop, and obsessively work on fixing it until I can unveil the perfect solution. It's the elephant-in-the-room syndrome—except I insist on wrestling that elephant alone until I can present it as a well-trained circus act.

Sound familiar? If you're like me, the big BUT problem boils down to four key phrases:

"I can't do this, BUT I'll do something else instead."

"I'll handle this quietly, BUT first, let me figure it out."

"I'll do what I think is best, BUT ask forgiveness later, knowing you won't agree with my solution."

"I'll tell you what I'm going to do, and if you say no, I'll go along with it, BUT I'll passive-aggressively resent you for a while."

The trouble with this approach? It doesn't work. The more I try to handle problems solo, the bigger and more overwhelming they become kind of like my actual butt after a late-night ice cream binge.

The Big BUT of "I'll Handle It Myself"

Here's the truth: I like to appear competent. Scratch that—I need to appear competent. If there's one thing my big BUT hates, it's letting people see me flounder.

Why admit I don't have a solution when I can quietly fix it and emerge victorious like some kind of crisis-solving ninja?

Unfortunately, this mindset tends to backfire. Why? Because while I'm busy trying to secretly tame my metaphorical elephant, it just keeps growing—and trampling everything in its path.

Take my email inbox (and let's face it, actual mail, too): I'll let messages pile into Mt. Kilimanjaro, convinced I'll create the perfect filing system. Instead, I end up paralyzed by indecision, then mark everything as read at once. (Pro tip: The 'archive all' button works as a quick 'I'll deal with this never' solution.)

The same thing happens with emotional or relational problems. I'll sit on my feelings, convincing myself I'll share them once I've sorted everything out. But by the time I'm ready to talk, the issue has usually spiraled into something much bigger than it needed to be. And there's a reason for this - several reasons, in fact. My big BUT isn't just being difficult; it's got some serious backup from my own brain.

The Science Behind My Big BUT (Or Why My Brain Won't Let Me Let Go)

Let's get nerdy for a minute, because there's some fascinating brain science behind why we get stuck in fix-it mode. Turns out, my big BUT isn't just being stubborn – it's my brain doing what brains do best: trying to keep me safe and in control (even when that control is totally an illusion).

Picture your brain as an overprotective parent at a playground. When it senses a problem, it doesn't just suggest a solution – it goes full helicopter mode. That's your prefrontal cortex lighting up like Times Square on New Year's Eve, screaming "Don't just stand there, DO SOMETHING!"

> sticky note to self
>
> Recognize when your "fixing" is creating more problems than solutions.

For those of us with neurodivergent brains, this gets even more interesting. Our brains don't just want to fix things – they NEED to fix things. It's like having an internal task manager permanently stuck in emergency mode, complete with flashing red lights and those annoying pop-up notifications that won't go away until you click them.

The Anxiety Amplifier

The Anxiety Amplifier shows up uninvited, turning everything up to eleven. It's like having an overeager assistant who keeps whispering (okay, sometimes shouting) "But what if...?" in your ear. Every potential problem becomes an emergency, and every emergency needs an immediate solution. RIGHT. NOW.

The Perfectionism Paradox

The Perfectionism Paradox is that indecisive friend who can't choose a restaurant without reading every single Yelp review—still scrolling while everyone else has finished dessert.

Perfectionists don't just want to fix problems; they want to solve them with surgical precision, ideally before they even exist. The cruel irony? This obsessive quest for the perfect solution breeds paralysis. We spin in endless mental circles, analyzing every possible approach until we're too exhausted to move. It's a marathon run on a hamster wheel—maximum effort, zero progress.

Sticky note to self

I tried to tame the elephant in the room by myself. Now we're both exhausted and the room is destroyed.

And just like that, our big BUT morphs into an even BIGGER BUT: 'But what if I can't fix it?' becomes 'But what if I'm fundamentally broken and no amount of fixing will ever be enough?' Garnish with anxiety and a generous sprinkle of paralyzing self-doubt.

However, if you want to go into sleuthing mode, you can see how the big BUT can be flipped in your favor simply in how you choose to verbalize what you are struggling with in the day-to-day. The 'But I'm broken and need fixing' transforms into 'But what if my brain is just wired differently?' Understanding this brain science stuff can be the first step to breaking free from the fix-it cycle. When we realize our brain is just doing its job—albeit a bit too enthusiastically—we can start to work with it

instead of against it. Recognizing why we default to fix-it mode is step one. Step two? Knowing when fixing becomes harmful.

When Fixing Becomes Harmful

The "fixer" mentality might feel like you're on top of things at first, but it quickly turns into a heavy burden. Here's how it goes:

Crisis Mode Exhaustion

Trying to fix everything, especially things that aren't yours to solve, is like swimming upstream through a river of cold molasses. You kick and struggle, but all you're doing is wearing yourself out for no good reason.

Tunnel Vision

When we get obsessed with fixing, we put horse blinders on and stampede toward what we think is the solution. We get so laser-focused on one tiny detail that we forget there's a whole world around us. Suddenly, all that matters is just having that one thing. It's the same reason I impulsively buy things—like when looking for a quick fix to make me feel better about life. Whether it's the innocuous string of Christmas lights I keep up in the house 365 days a year, or allowing myself to spend way too much time making my Amazon shopping cart full of things I've placed on my Pinterest boards, I zero in on what will make the world in front of my eyes easier, without even reading the fine print. That immediate satisfaction sometimes feels good, and sometimes, it feels like, "Why was I so stupid to think I'd get a $5 full-sized Rolls Royce from Temu?"

Strained Relationships

Now, here's the real kicker—this whole "fix-it-all" thing doesn't just mess with your own head. It messes with everyone around you, too—especially the people who genuinely want to support our mental health journey. We often don't realize how much pressure we're putting on them.

Exhibit B: My furnace pilot light went out, and I needed Philip's help. But guiding me over FaceTime with his vision impairment was challenging. Instead of patiently waiting for him to find the right instructions, I decided to take matters into my own hands. I shoved my arm into the back of the furnace, feeling around for the button only to realize I couldn't pull it back out. After much struggling, I finally yanked my arm free—scraped up and sporting a very fashionable shade of black and blue.

sticky note to self

My inbox reached epic status. So I marked everything as read and called it a filing system.

But here's the twist: I didn't just leave with a bruised arm. I left with Philip's bruised spirit. My impatience wasn't just physical—it was relational. I was so desperate to control the situation that I couldn't see what was right in front of me: a husband trying to help. He was patiently guiding me through something he couldn't even see, and I treated him like an obstacle. Eventually, I called my brother-in-law Robbie over who actually knew what he was doing (the same guy Philip had asked me to call in the first place, but nooo, I HAD to figure it out myself). He fixed it in less than five minutes and also changed out my clogged up return vent that wasn't helping the situation.

When we get stuck in our need to control, we forget that the people who care for us have their own vulnerabilities. It's mentally harmful to those who care for us, leaving them feeling unheard, dismissed, and invisible.

Living Proof: The Tom Effect

Let me tell you about one of the greatest gifts I've ever received. It came from a man I lovingly call my "second dad"—Tom, who along with his wife Dorcas, showed me what it truly means to let go of my big BUT and accept help.

When I met Tom in 1978, I was a wide-eyed five-year-old visiting my dad at work. Dad was a typesetter at Gospel Publishing House, and Tom was a young Bible college student working as a stripper—of prepress negatives, that is. (He still gets a kick out of telling people that one!)

After I graduated from college, I eventually became the youth magazine editor at the same publishing house. It was in that place that Tom became more than a colleague. He was my mentor, sounding board, and cheerleader—with an endless supply of M&Ms stashed in his office. When I needed to vent, he'd listen, offer encouragement, and send me back into the fray with a clearer head and some much-needed chocolate.

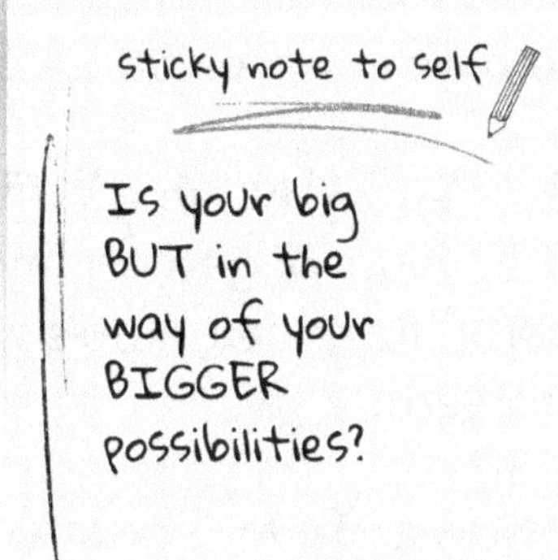

But it was during one of my biggest challenges that Tom taught me the most powerful lesson about accepting help. I'd been handed the "opportunity" to launch a new women's magazine, *Leading Hearts,* with zero staff and resources. It was the kind of situation that typically sent my fix-it instincts into overdrive.

That's when Tom made an offer that still brings tears to my eyes: "I want to take care of the things you don't do best so you can focus on the things you do best. I want Amber to do what only Amber can do."

And he meant it. He became my volunteer copy editor, advisor, and all-around helper for the Advanced Writers and Speakers Association—where he remains the token guy in our AWSA sisterhood of 1000-plus Christian women communicators.

Tom's unwavering support taught me something crucial: sometimes the bravest thing we can do is let someone else help carry our load. His gift wasn't just about editing or handling tasks—it was permission to stop trying to do it all alone.

So, who are the Toms in your life? Who has shown up, offering their strengths to support your journey? Consider writing them a note of gratitude. Then look around—is there someone in your circle who needs you to be their Tom? Sometimes honoring the help we've received means passing it forward.

Shrinking the Big BUT: Solutions That Actually Work

After years of getting my arm stuck in metaphorical (and literal) furnaces, here's what I've learned about my big BUT problem:

1. Name Your Struggles

sticky note to self

Maybe you are concerning yourself with a solution someone else is meant to find. Don't steal their opportunity.

When I finally said out loud, "I'm overwhelmed with work and need help," something shifted. Those words lifted weight I didn't even know I was carrying. Turns out, naming the problem doesn't make you weak—it just makes the problem smaller.

2. Hit the Pause Button

I've started asking myself three questions before launching into fix-it mode: Is this my problem to solve? Does it need solving RIGHT NOW? Am I responding from fear or wisdom? This pause has saved me from so many impulsive decisions. (RIP, turkey neck massager. You deserved better than a life in my junk drawer).

3. Embrace Collaboration

Tom taught me this: Even Batman has Robin. Even Wonder Woman has her Amazonian sisters. Asking for help isn't surrender—it's strategy. "I want Amber to do what only Amber can do" meant I had to let go of everything else. Turns out, collaboration makes you stronger, not weaker.

4. Choose Depth Over Quick Fixes

Quick fixes are tempting. They're like slapping a Band-Aid on a broken bone—might cover the surface, but it doesn't touch the root cause. I learned this the hard way when I reorganized my spice rack instead of addressing a work deadline. Alphabetized anxiety is still anxiety.

5. Welcome Imperfection

"Done is better than perfect" became my mantra after I rewrote the same email seventeen times and still didn't send it. Sometimes "good enough" isn't just acceptable—it's optimal. When I stopped chasing perfection, I actually started finishing things.

6. Create Safe Spaces

I needed spaces where I could fail without harsh self-criticism. Where I could admit I don't have all the answers. Where "I don't know" is a complete sentence. These spaces became laboratories for growth—mistakes transformed from stumbling blocks into stepping stones.

Each strategy builds on the others. The goal isn't eliminating all challenges overnight—it's developing healthier approaches. Transformation isn't about perfect execution; it's about showing up consistently, leaning on support systems, and extending grace.

Finding the Humor in It All

Here's the thing about having a big BUT problem: It's funny. Truly. Once you step back and see the absurdity, you can't help but laugh. Laugh at the times you've rewritten the same email seventeen times, sent nothing, and then the problem resolved itself anyway.

Laugh at the times your "quick fix" created three new problems that required their own quick fixes.

Laugh at the times you've been so busy solving an imaginary future crisis that you missed the actual present moment entirely.

Because here's what I've learned: the ability to laugh at your own big BUT is actually the beginning of letting it go. You can't take something too seriously and release it at the same time. Humor is the exhale that loosens the grip of control.

Honestly, some of my best fix-it fails start with "I watched a YouTube tutorial…"

I continually have to stop myself in my tracks when my fixer addiction wants to rear its head. It is not my job in life to redeem everything that goes south. For me, that trust looks like faith—believing there is a better plan beyond my control than anything I could contrive in my frantic fixing. The point is learning to let go of the illusion that you have to control everything. I spend each day reminding myself that I don't have enough life to spend it micromanaging the outcome.

Letting Go of the Big BUT

Here's the thing about our big BUTs—they don't define us. They're just chapters in a much bigger story. And the ultimate plot twist? Learning that we don't have to fix everything ourselves. That's been my game changer, and I learn more about this every day.

When I let go and surrender to the messy whatever-will-bes in my life, something remarkable happens: those struggles, missteps, and even the biggest BUTs transform into stepping stones toward something more amazing than I could have imagined.

We are welcoming mental breakdown if we allow Ms. Fix-It to rule our mind and run our bodies into the ground . For me, that lesson came through faith—and knowing some of those paths I was never meant to bulldoze in my own power. For you, it might look like leaning on community, trusting therapy, or simply accepting uncertainty as part of what it means to be human.

This truth takes all that pressure of perfection and control and shifts it—above us, to trusted people, or to the acceptance that we don't have to have all the answers. We're stronger when we stop trying to carry every burden alone.

I've learned to face whatever comes with faith, grace, and yes— maybe even a little looser-fitting jeans.

#shortyellowpencilRX—Your Daily Dose

"Can YOU fix it? No, Don't Even Try!!!" When was the last time your "fix-it" plan went completely sideways. How did your brilliant solution end up costing you more? What did you learn about letting go, asking for help, or embracing imperfection?

PAGE TURNER

Honestly, there's one more big BUT lurking in the shadows: "Everything is amazing for everyone else, BUT me." That's Eeyore's signature move. He's been perfecting this victim mentality since the Hundred Acre Wood opened for business, and he's been stubbornly holding onto it like the... well, donkey he is. When we're standing in our puddles watching everyone else's highlight reels, that BUT becomes our whole personality. So before you drown in ankle-deep water while everyone else floats by, let's talk about perspective, puddles, and pink inflatable birds.

RANDOM DOODLE SPACE

Emergency Preparedness

Level: Mildly Damp

CHAPTER 9

Shutting Up Your Inner Eeyore
(Learning to Float on Life's Puddles)

"Thanks for noticing me."

Does this voice sound familiar? I'm quite acquainted with this donkey from childhood, and sometimes he returns to be my inner monologue. How about you?

We're talking about Eeyore from Winnie the Pooh—that perpetually gloomy donkey convinced his tail is gonna fall off and nobody likes him and it's probably specifically gonna rain on his parade.

There's a song I heard this morning—"Why Does It Always Rain on Me?" by the artist Travis—and I was like, oh my gosh, this is the most depressing song ever. Eeyore needs to totally be the backup singer on this.

When Did We All Become Eeyore?

So here's what I'm seeing everywhere: we have normalized a victim mentality where everything is conspiring against us, everything is holding us down, holding us back. We're convinced we're perpetually underwater, that nothing will ever be quite right. And COVID turned us all into Eeyores.

Suddenly, everyone had a legitimate reason to believe everything was going wrong, nothing would ever be normal again. And some of us (including yours truly) were just waiting for the next bad thing to drop. Honestly, I was on the look out for gangs of gun-toting seagulls.

But here's what I realized: people look at a puddle and act like they're drowning. They're wading in the kiddie pool and calling it an ocean. They're standing in the middle of a mud puddle acting like they need a life raft.

The Mess We're In (And the One We're Not)

Now we live in a paradox here. We have to acknowledge the things that aren't going well. If we don't, we're living in fantasy land, right?

We can't just pretend everything is fine, either. That's not faith, that is denial.

But here's the other side: if we don't recognize the goodness, if we can't see the beauty still present in our lives, how in the world are we ever gonna be happy? How are we ever going to find joy?

Because here's the hard truth: you create the atmosphere and you bring it with you.

Think about it. When people come into your space, what do they feel? Do they feel sunshine, joy, gratitude? Or do they feel like they've just walked into a complaint convention where everything casts shade in every direction?

How Pink Inflatable Birds Became My Life Raft

During quarantine, I looked around at the chaos and thought, "I need to improve this space we're all stuck in." And somehow my brain landed on flamingos. Specifically, floating flamingos.

Why flamingos? Because they're ridiculous, hilarious, and we desperately needed some ridiculous, hilarious nonsense. Plus, if you think about it, flamingos are basically the life coaches we all need. They're awkward—those knees look like they might buckle any second. They're resilient—thriving in swampy, messy conditions without complaint. And they're unapologetically fabulous—strutting around in hot pink without a care in the world.

If flamingos can look glamorous standing ankle-deep in brown sludge, I figured I could survive a global pandemic.

So I went ALL IN. I created The Flamingo Floaty Tribe—a virtual lazy river where my girlfriends and I could float on the backs of inflatable pink majestic birds through the chaos together. I designed a mascot. I held a contest to name her. My sister-in-law Minda won, and we christened our pink queen "Tilly." She stood proudly on a little blue floaty with the tagline "Just Floating Through," and that became our entire pandemic personality.

I made custom graphics with Tilly's logo. I created t-shirts and gave them away like they were COVID vaccines. I designed memes. I threw a virtual luau complete with a flamingo giveaway and had everyone dress in pink just to be ridiculous. That tribe of 90 people started flooding the group with pink joy—every funny meme, every ridiculous flamingo cake, photos of flamingo cars, pictures snapped in the Hobby Lobby flamingo aisle. It was glorious, chaotic nonsense.

Our motto? "Be a flamingo in a flock of pigeons." Because flamingos don't try to blend in. They stand tall in their awkward fabulousness, and that's exactly the energy we needed when we were stuck in the muck.

MO' Parties in the Puddle Coves

Now I need to tell you about something that happens in my hometown of Springfield, Missouri that perfectly captures the spirit of choosing joy in ridiculous circumstances. You know how kids love puddle jumping? Well, my hometown has taken puddle jumping to a whole new level—we're talking puddle rafting.

During flash flood season, giant puddles form in Westport Park. It's the place I used to play in as a kid (and yes, to my mother's dismay, I used to crawl through its under-road drainage cavern). But now the deep resevoir that was built in my adult years holds a substantial body of temporary water. And I've seen people, I kid you not, treat them like the party cove at Lake of the Ozarks.

They show up with inflatable rafts. They bring coolers. They wade in with pool noodles and beach balls. These folks are out there in random runoff puddles, living their best lives like they've just scored lakefront property.

Now, let me be clear. Am I condoning hanging out in flash flood drainage that might have who-knows-what bacteria or could suck you down into a drainage ditch? Absolutely not. There's real potential hazard there. But watching these people make the best of literal muddy water? I found it both hilarious and honestly kind of beautiful. These weren't people in denial. They knew they were standing in a park puddles. They knew it wasn't Lake Como. But they made a choice: they could stand on the sidelines complaining about the flooding, or they could grab a flamingo floaty and make it a party.

They weren't waiting for perfect circumstances. They were choosing joy in the mess of the flood. They were floating instead of drowning.

That image stuck with me. Because isn't that what we're all doing? We're all standing in some version of a puddle—whether it's a difficult season, a challenging relationship, a career setback, or a global pandemic. The question isn't whether the puddle exists. The question is, are you going to drown in it, or are you going to float?

That became my whole vibe, my survival mantra, my pandemic thesis statement: I'd rather float on a puddle than sink in the rain.

The Flamingo Floaty Prescription

So what's the medicine for that Eeyore complex living rent-free in your head? Here's what you need to do:

Stop Calling for a Life Raft in Ankle-Deep Water

This is the big one, friends. Stop catastrophizing. Stop treating every puddle like an ocean. Some of you need to hear this with the kind of brutal honesty that good friends tell each other:

sticky note to self

You can't help inflate someone else's floaty when your drowning in self-pity.

You are not drowning. You're standing in ankle-deep water acting like you need CPR.

The problem is real, but your commentary is making it a crisis.

Get. Some. Perspective.

Here's what I mean: Yes, your car broke down. That's frustrating. But you're not stranded on a deserted island. Yes, your kid failed a test. That's disappointing. But they're not flunking out of life. Yes, you had a hard day at work. That's exhausting. But you're not in a Dickensian workhouse. Learn to distinguish between a genuine tsunami and a splash from a passing car. Your mental health depends on it.

You're Either Stewing in Soup or Sewage

Your words aren't neutral—they're either medicine or toxicity. Every single thing you say about yourself and your situation is either offering nourishment or creating a toxic run-off. You are literally creating your reality with your mouth, and some of you are talking yourself into a deep trench you didn't need to dig.

So what words that you might be saying that are making your situation worse? How are you making your weather more bleak with your own commentary? Because here's the truth that sounds harsh but will set you free: you create the atmosphere and you bring it with you.

Think about it. Are you the person who walks into a room and people's shoulders relax, or are you the person who walks in and people brace themselves?

This isn't about toxic positivity or pretending everything's fine. This is about recognizing that your words have power, and you get to choose how you wield that power over yourself and others who come into your space. And maybe, just maybe your circle of friends is non-existent because the dark which has become your comfortable space is just too overwhelming. That, friends, is a state of mindfulness. You alone have the control to open the window of new perspective and let fresh breeze in— even if it is only one inch at a time. Every tiny move up—that's progress.

What's Keeping You Buoyant?

What keeps you afloat? What are the practices, people, and small moments of light that prevent you from going under? For me, it was community, humor, and choosing joy even when it felt impossible. It was surrounding myself with people who amplified my joy instead of dulling my sparkle. It was literally creating joy—from designing graphics to making t-shirts to throwing ridiculous virtual parties.

Here's what I discovered: when you're actively looking for ways to bring sunshine into someone else's storm, you cannot stay stuck in your own mess. Giving away joy became as much of a gift to me as it was to them.

So find your floaties. Maybe it's a group chat that makes you laugh. Maybe it's a hobby that lights you up. Maybe it's volunteering, creating, moving your body, or simply choosing to notice three good things every day. Whatever keeps you buoyant, do more of that. Protect it. Prioritize it. Because you can't pour from an empty cup, and you can't float without your floaties.

The Muck Moves Downstream

There's an ancient story about a guy named Job who lost everything—and I mean everything. But there's this one line that stuck with me: "You will surely forget your trouble, recalling it only as waters gone by" (Job 11:16, NIV).

At first I thought, forget my troubles? How? But then I got it. Trouble is temporary. It flows past like water downstream. The muck you're standing in now won't last forever. And while you're waiting for the waters to clear, you can choose to float.

This isn't about denying reality. This isn't about pretending the puddle doesn't exist. This is about recognizing that trouble is temporary, and your response to it doesn't have to be permanent despair. You can acknowledge the mess while refusing to set up camp in it. You can say, "Yes, this is hard" without also saying, "And therefore my life is over."

Where in the Water Are You?

So here's my challenge, and I want you to really sit with this:

What puddle are you standing in right now that you're treating like an ocean?

What words are you speaking over yourself that are making things worse instead of better?

What would it look like to choose, today, to float instead of sink?

Put a flamingo floaty on the mud puddle of life. You don't need to fix everything. You don't need to drain the puddle. You just need to stop drowning in it.

You don't have to wait for the storm to pass to laugh—you can float right through it. And here's the beautiful secret: when you choose to be a flamingo in a flock of pigeons, when you decide to bring your own weather, when you refuse to let the puddle become your identity—you give everyone around you permission to do the same.

That's the real gift. That's the legacy. That's what this whole journey is about.

#shortyellowpencilRX—Your Daily Dose

What puddle are you currently standing in that you're treating like an ocean? Write it down. Now, what would your "flamingo floaty" look like for that situation? What's one small thing you could do today to choose floating over drowning? Think about those possibilities and include those thoughts here.

PAGE TURNER

Before you turn the page, grab your toasting skewer... because when the world becomes a dumpster fire (and let's be honest, it has been), you need a survival strategy. Mine? Emotional support marshmallows—you're welcome to take a seat round the pit.

RANDOM DOODLE SPACE

RANDOM DOODLE SPACE

Tired of Feelin' the Ridulous Heat?

Perfectly Toast Your Favorite Treat

When the World Hands You a Dumpster Fire,
(Toast Some Marshmallows)

For the past few months, I've felt a sinking sensation, as though an overwhelming urge to close off the world has been steadily creeping in. There's been this quiet urge to put the shutters up on life, to shield myself from whatever the future may bring. The uncertainty often feels like too much to bear.

And sometimes, it's not just a bad day—it's a full-blown dumpster fire that drags on for a week, a month, or even longer. You know the kind I'm talking about—when everything feels like it's spiraling out of control. The smoke of chaos clouds your thoughts, and the heat of the flames threatens to overwhelm you. You're so kicked in your spirit, you feel like a deflated party balloon—forgotten on the floor while everyone steps over you. That's when I discovered an unlikely source of comfort: marshmallows. More specifically, a new life-guiding principle: When the world hands you a dumpster fire, toast some marshmallows.

Now, you might be wondering what on earth I mean by that. It all started one evening when I decided to step outside and do something small but peaceful: I set out to fish for the catch of the day—a perfectly toasted jumbo campfire marshmallow using an absurdly long, five-foot toasting skewer over my fire pit. Some people find joy in fishing; for me, it became marshmallow fishing. Same calming process—minus the baited hooks, wet clothes, or risk of capsizing. What started as a simple, silly activity became a surprisingly powerful tool to recalibrate my mindset and find peace.

The Art of Fishing for Marshmallows

You see, toasting marshmallows isn't just about getting them golden brown. It's about mindfulness. I carefully hold each fat marshmallow over the flame, slowly rotating it until every side is evenly toasted. I focus solely on this task, letting the rest of the world slip away. It's methodical. The heat from the flame creates a soft glow in the air, and I settle into the warmth. As the marshmallow slowly browns, I notice how my mind clears. My worries and the day's stress just fade into the background.

Slowly hovering that toasting fork above the glow of that fire pit is the most peaceful thirty minutes of my day. It's just me, the flame, and the marshmallow. I don't rush through it (so you can see why normal-sized marshmallows won't do). The simple act of focusing on something small, something calming, has become my way of finding peace in the chaos. In this place, life isn't a dumpster fire. It's just quiet stillness and gratitude for this oasis.

And no, I don't eat the marshmallows. I carefully toast them to perfection, then give them away—often to my family or occasionally to my dogs (though they end up with white sticky fur). It's not about the marshmallow itself but the process: focusing on the dispersal of stress to something that is methodically peaceful, taking in the immediate sweetness of the world right in front of my face.

Your Campfire in the Chaos

One of the many quotes I have hanging in my kitchen is from Henry David Thoreau's book *Walden*: "That man is the richest whose pleasures are the cheapest." Why am I telling you this? Because it speaks to the heart of mental health and the struggles we all face. Life often feels chaotic, especially when focusing solely on what's going wrong. We can get so caught up in the dumpster fire that we fail to notice the simple, beautiful moments that can help us reset our minds and hearts.

I want to challenge you to find your version of "fishing for marshmallows." Maybe it's watching the sunset, reading a chapter of your favorite book, or even taking a quiet walk. It doesn't matter what it is, as long as it lets you step away from the dumpster momentarily. You know what's wild? How easy it is to suffocate inside your own head. We replay conversations that are over. Rehearse arguments that'll never happen. Catastrophize outcomes that haven't occurred. Then we sit in those pits wondering why we feel stuck.

sticky note to self

Even dumpster fires make great s'mores— just don't forget the chocolate!

I've learned that in the mess of life, we need to focus on goodness, childlike wonder, and appreciate the simplest things.

Those flickers of light from the fire pit remind me that every good thing in my life isn't going up in smoke.

It's about changing our focus, not ignoring the dumpster fire, but looking for the light that shines even when everything else is in flames.

That brings me to the idea of light. Like a campfire in the dark, there is always light in the chaos of life. We can't always control the flames of the dumpster fire, but we can choose where we focus our eyes. And sometimes, all we need is to turn our gaze to something new.

I've found strength in remembering that, even in the dark times, there's always something to help guide me through. For me, it's confidence in the light, even if I can't see it. So, when standing in the middle of your dumpster fire, remember that you don't need to have it all figured out before you find a glimmer of joy. Just take the next step, and many times that step is found in creating space for rest.

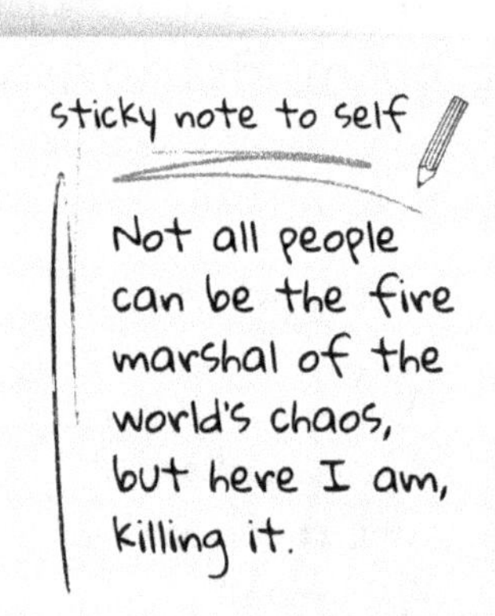

When the Smoke Overtakes You

Sometimes, life just stinks. It's unfair, exhausting, and overwhelming—like standing in the middle of a fire that threatens to consume everything around you. The smoke clouds your vision, the heat drains your energy, and it feels like there's no way out.

But I've learned something powerful: when I focus on what's right—however small or fleeting—I feel a shift.

Whether it's a quiet prayer, a peaceful marshmallow toasting session, or simply taking a deep breath, those tiny sparks of light help me navigate the chaos.

We don't have to pretend everything is fine when it's not. It's okay to admit life is hard and that the dumpster fire feels like too much to handle. Some days, survival is the only goal—and that's okay.

On those days, thriving isn't even on the table. It's about getting through—no more, no less. These small steps have helped me hold steady when the flames feel like they're closing in:

Survival Mode: A Field Guide

Ugly Cry Your Mascara Off—Cry. The kind where your face gets blotchy and you go through half a tissue box. Tears aren't weakness—they're release. Sometimes the only way forward is to feel the full weight of something so you can actually begin to let it go. So grab the tissues, let it all out, and don't apologize for it.

Let Your Feet Feel Some Dirt—When everything feels like it's spinning out of control, focus on something tangible. Actually go outside and stand barefoot in the grass if you can. Or wrap your hands around a warm mug and feel the heat seep into your palms. Count your breaths—in for four, out for four. These grounding techniques aren't magic, but they remind you that you're here, right now, and you're safe.

Make It Stupidly Small—Think ridiculously small. Eat cereal for dinner. Watch a dumb TV show and actually laugh. Stand in a hot shower until the water runs cold. Survival mode isn't about peak performance—it's about giving yourself room to just breathe. Let go of the unnecessary expectations. Permission granted: focus on the basics.

Zone Out on Purpose—Give yourself permission to completely check out for a bit. Watch ridiculous cat videos. Make memes in Canva. Go take pictures of literally anything outside. Reread your favorite book for the hundredth time. Take a nap in the middle of the day like a toddler. This isn't avoidance—it's giving your brain a break from the constant smoke inhalation. If you work from home like me, these mental vacations aren't optional—they're survival. Try to do it at the same time every day if you can, but honestly? Just do it whenever the fire feels too close.

Set Goals a Toddler Could Handle—Today's goal might literally be: don't throw your phone against the wall. Or maybe it's: brush your teeth. Get out of bed before noon. Drink a glass of water instead of downing a two-liter of your favorite caffeinated beverage. These aren't pathetic—they're victories when you're in survival mode. Celebrate them like you just won the lottery, because when everything feels like an uphill battle in hiking boots two sizes too small, these tiny wins are what keep you moving forward. Progress doesn't always look impressive. Sometimes it just looks like you made it through another day.

Just Handle the Next Five Minutes—Focus on the next five minutes—not the next five days, weeks, or months. Break time into bite-sized pieces so small they almost don't matter, and deal only with what's directly in front of you right this second. When your brain tries to spiral into next week's disasters or replay last month's failures on loop, drag it back. Gently if you can, forcefully if you have to. What does the next five minutes need from you? A glass of water? Three deep breaths? To sit down and stare at the wall? Just that. Nothing more. When everything feels overwhelming and the fire seems endless, staying present keeps it from growing bigger in your mind than it actually is in reality.

Don't Try to Figure It Out—Struggle and hope can coexist. Pain and faith can sit in the same room without one canceling out the other. You don't have to reconcile it all or make it make sense.

For me, it's often hanging on by a singular thought—"God is with me" is its own kind of victory. My faith doesn't erase the fire, but it reminds me I'm not walking through it alone.

For you, maybe you're holding onto the fact that you've survived 100% of your worst days so far. Or knowing there's someone you can call when it gets too heavy. Or trusting that feelings pass even when they feel permanent. Or a song lyric, a quote, a memory of better days.

The point isn't what you hold onto. The point is holding onto something—anything of goodness—when the smoke is so thick you can barely breathe.

Scream Into the Void (No Filter, No Apologies)—Pour it all out—honestly, messily, completely. Whether you scream it to God, yell it into actual nothing, or write it in a journal that no one will ever read, just get it out.

Chicago literally had a "Scream into the Void" event where people stood by Lake Michigan and screamed. No filter. No apologies. All the raw feelings straight into the open air.

For me, I talk to God unfiltered. I've ugly cried. I've cussed. I've demanded answers He hasn't given. Even when those answers don't come, I find comfort knowing I'm not in the stench and heat of my dumpster reality alone.

But maybe your version is writing it all in a journal and burning the pages. Or recording a voice memo and deleting it. Or finding your own scream spot—Lake Michigan optional. Or talking to a friend who knows how to just listen.

The point is just pushing everything flammable, those things that can take you down, out of your head and back INTO the world where they belong. Because when you let everything suffocate inside your own skull, you can't look up and see there's still sky above the smoke.

sticky note to self

Many times in the firestorm of opinion your the one who ends up burnt. Don't invest in them.

Find the Marshmallows in the Chaos

Life is hard. The world is a mess. And some of us have to dig way deeper than others to find the good stuff.

Between the news cycle, personal crises, global disasters, and your own daily struggles, it can feel like everything is burning all at once. The world's on fire. Your life's on fire. Sometimes it's hard to tell where one fire ends and the other begins.

But here's what I've learned: even when everything feels like it's going up in flames—both out there and in here—you can still look for the small things that remind you the fire doesn't get the final say.

Those things I look for may be tiny, but they are tangible. A cozy blanket. A perfectly toasted marshmallow. The smell of clean laundry. The way the light hits the trees in the morning. A stupid meme that makes me laugh when the news is too heavy. These aren't distractions from the fire—they're reminders that beauty and joy still exist even when everything else is burning.

I'm not saying to ignore the dumpster fires—personal or global. I'm not saying to stick your head in the sand and pretend everything's fine. I'm saying: while you're standing in the smoke, look for the small joys. They anchor you. They remind you that life is more than the crisis you're currently in or the disaster currently unfolding on your screen.

And when the fire gets too loud and too hot? Laugh at something ridiculous. Watch a stupid video. Find something absurd and let yourself crack up about it. Laughter is a fire extinguisher for the soul. It doesn't put out the flames, but it gives you enough breathing room to keep going.

Life's heat—both yours and the world's—doesn't have to destroy you. It can refine you. You don't have to like the fire. You don't have to be grateful for it. But you can look for the marshmallows in the middle of it. Or better yet, the crème brûlée.

#shortyellowpencilRX—Your Daily Dose

Think about your personal marshmallow-toasting activity—the thing that grounds you when life feels like it's burning down around you. What's your version? Taking pictures outside? Making memes in Canva? Standing barefoot in the grass?

PAGE TURNER

If you've just put marshmallows on your shopping list, kudos. You've just taken the first step towards improving your mental health. But speaking of heat, for all of us ladies who know there's nothing like getting to the age where your own body turns into a menopausal furnace. And if you haven't seen the viral video of the woman in the dead of winter with visible steam rising from her bald head, you need to google it immediately. I can relate to the power of those hot flashes—especially when they come paired with the world's most annoying hold music. So after you're finished on YouTube, I'll meet you over in the next chapter.

RANDOM DOODLE SPACE

RANDOM DOODLE SPACE

RANDOM DOODLE SPACE

The De-Evolution of Hold Music

Chapter 11

Stuck in Hold Music Purgatory
(This Call May Be Monitored
While Your Patience Falls Apart)

Let's talk about the unique hell that is hold music purgatory.

Imagine three hours—three hours—of tinny, looping music that sounds like it was composed by someone who got rejected from jingle school. Add to that a robotic voice popping in every two minutes to tell you, "Your call is important to us."

Really? Is it, though? Because if it were actually important, I wouldn't have aged a full year waiting for someone to answer. At this point, I half-expected them to say, "Your call is important to us … but not as important as our extended lunch break."

This particular nightmare was courtesy of the IRS. I'd like to tell you I handled it with calm and grace, but the truth is, I was one disconnected call away from a full-on meltdown. My blood pressure was climbing. My patience had packed its bags and left hours ago. And I was about thirty seconds away from snapping at my dog Stanley, who had the audacity to paw at my arm for attention while I was clearly suffering.

And just when I thought I couldn't take it anymore, the line went dead.

I sat there staring at the phone like it had personally betrayed me. The silence was louder than any hold music.

Stress Doesn't Just Show Up—It Moves In

Stress is like that uninvited guest who shows up, overstays their welcome, and raids your fridge while they're at it. One minute, you're just trying to call the IRS, and the next, you're spiraling into a full-blown panic attack. Stress doesn't just mess with your mind—it hijacks your focus and refuses to let go.

Suddenly, your world revolves around tinny elevator music, and everything else—your to-do list, grocery plans, and ability to function—vanishes into the void. Stress doesn't stop there, though. It brings along its buddies: headaches, stomachaches, and a laundry list of symptoms designed to ruin your day.

Worse yet, stress doesn't just take over your body—it turns you into a one-person wrecking crew. Every tiny inconvenience feels catastrophic. The poor soul who innocently asks, "What's for dinner?" becomes an unwitting target of your wrath. And the IRS? They're not just a tax agency; they're now your arch-nemesis. But here's the truth: it's not the IRS, the hold music, or the missed dinner. It's the weight of unprocessed tension bubbling up and exploding at the wrong target.

Recognize this isn't about justifying your outbursts. It's about catching yourself before the eruption and asking, "Is this really the problem—or am I just carrying too much?" Spoiler alert: it's usually the latter.

sticky note to self

Don't give stress the power to scribble all over your day.

That's when it's time to pause, breathe, and recalibrate—before someone else becomes collateral damage in your stress-fueled hurricane. Take time to recall: How many times have you found yourself completely overreacting to something small, only to realize later that it wasn't the situation—it was the stress you were already carrying? Yeah, we've all been there. Now, let's move on to the battle plan.

Feed Your Face Before You Lose It

Here's the thing: I'm no expert on nutrition, and I'm not here to give you a doctor's degree in dietetics. I'm sharing what I've learned through trial and error—and maybe some personal pain. Have you ever tried to tackle stress when your stomach feels like it's eating itself? You know, when you're "hangry"? Yeah, that's not a good combo.

> I can feel my stomach baring its fangs—and it will take a bite of someone—anyone, in its path.

There's something that happens when you don't eat enough: Suddenly, every small problem feels like it's a catastrophe. Amid my epic IRS hold music disaster, I realized—Oh, no. I haven't eaten anything all day. No wonder I felt like my entire world was crashing down around me!

I'm not saying you must go on a full-blown food crusade and become a snack expert. But if you're about to face a stressful situation, it's probably not the best idea to do it on an empty stomach. A handful of something (I don't care if it's nuts, fruit, or the leftover granola bar you forgot you had) can help stabilize your mood just enough to keep the panic at bay. The last thing you want is for the stress to turn into a full-on emotional rollercoaster because you didn't bother to eat.

Keep a snack in your bag or desk. It won't solve your IRS woes, but it might help keep you from having a mental breakdown over hold music.

Drink Water Before You Implode

Did you know that dehydration can make stress worse? I didn't, either, until I was on hold for so long that I forgot to drink water. I was dehydrated, stressed, and probably one deep breath away from screaming at the automated voice to just please connect me to a real person. That's when it hit me: My heart was racing, my head was pounding, and I was ready to implode. Then, I realized it wasn't just stress—I was running on empty. My body needed water.

> I'm not saying water will solve all your problems, but I can promise you that it can make a difference in how you handle stress.

So, before you yell at your spouse or bark at the dogs for daring to interrupt your "me time," take a sip of water. It won't hurt, I promise. If anything, it might give you just the little bit of clarity you need to stop yourself from going full-on meltdown mode. And even though you might be tempted to, refrain from grabbing that three-week-old soda in your car's cup holder. Remember, your body, made up of 55-60% water, needs more water than food to survive. Stay hydrated, stay calm, and remember: nobody wins when you're dehydrated and stressed out.

When Stress Sucks the Life Out of You

Okay, so stress messes with our minds, our bodies, and our ability to function as normal human beings. But here's the kicker—stress is an energy vampire. It sucks the life out of you, especially when you're on that endless loop of frustration (or hold music). Your body floods your system with cortisol, and suddenly, you're running on fumes.

You're so mentally deflated by the situation that you just want to curl up in a ball and pretend you're no longer part of the real world. Wouldn't it be nice to just check out for a while? Instead, you find yourself stuck in the weird vortex of stress that has you questioning every life decision you've ever made.

Here's what I've learned: when stress has sucked the last ounce of energy out of you, the best thing you can do is rest. I'm not talking about taking a five-minute break and calling it a day. I mean a real break—whether getting some sleep or taking time to fill your lungs with air and reset. Stress is a marathon, not a sprint, and if you're feeling like a toddler who's been awake for forty-eight hours straight, it's time to hit pause.

Don't Be the Stressed T-Rex

We've all been there—stress makes you take it out on the ones you love. You snap at your spouse over something completely trivial or bark at your kids for interrupting you while trying to survive a phone call with customer service. It's embarrassing and hard to admit when you've lost your temper. But here's the reality: stress doesn't discriminate. It makes you irritable, and when you're already on edge, the people closest to you become the easiest target for your frustration.

So, what do you do? How do you stop yourself from being the stressed T-Rex?

Know When Stress Is Doing the Talking

Start by recognizing that the issue may not be the person in front of you—the stress inside you is talking. Are you snapping because of a minor inconvenience, or is your mind just overwhelmed by everything? Taking a breath and recognizing the source of your frustration is half the battle.

Actually Apologize Like an Adult

After you've snapped, it's time to apologize. Say, "Hey, I'm sorry. I'm overwhelmed right now and didn't handle that well." This is humble and honest, allowing you to reset the conversation.

Give People a Heads-Up

If you know stress is brewing, let the people around you know. "I'm feeling overwhelmed right now, so this is not the best time to talk. I need to rest my mind." Just communicating what's going on can prevent the fallout from taking over.

Find Your Timeout Corner

Step away when stress is about to burst. Whether going for a walk, taking a bathroom break, or locking yourself in the car for five minutes—just take a breather. It's okay to step away and return to things when you're not in danger of blowing up. Sometimes I'm pushing through work and I won't even reward myself with a bathroom break. I'm literally toxifying my body by refusing to get up for a few minutes until I finish the task in front of me. How crazy is that?

Push That Boulder Out of Your Way

This sounds weird, but it works: imagine your stress as a massive boulder blocking your path. Picture yourself standing in front of it. Take a deep breath, put your hands out, plant your feet, activate your core, and push. Push hard. Keep pushing until you visualize it rolling out of your way. You'll be surprised at how well this works to relieve stress.

There's No Magic Fix

Stress is a tough cookie, but it is inevitable—you will face stressful, anxiety-inducing situations daily. Tackling a pile of it at once when your brain is maxed out is no easy feat. But with some hydration, a snack here and there (without calling yourself a nutrition expert), and a little self-awareness, you can handle it like a pro—without losing your cool and sense of humor. Keep breathing, keep sipping, and remember: hold music is just a temporary inconvenience. Stress will always try to claim all the real estate you give it. It likes to roam and run amock, ruining every inch of your peace. The real trick is wrangling it and refusing to let it run the show.

Hold Music PTSD Is Actually a Thing

Let's talk about hold music PTSD. You know exactly what I mean if you've ever spent hours on the phone with lousy music looping in your ear. Every time I hear something similar, my body tenses up, my heart races, and I'm transported back to frustration and helplessness.

It sounds ridiculous, but it's real. All stressors that we experience in life can leave a mark—even if the source seems silly in hindsight. Your body remembers what you long to move past because it secretly tells you, "This will go down just like it did way back when." The key is acknowledging

sticky note to self

Apologize quickly because your humanity needs just as much grace as others do.

those feelings and giving yourself the grace to acknowledge what you are feeling and do what it takes to cope healthily with that stressor without losing your sanity.

Managing the Madness

Stress doesn't disappear with a snack or a sip of water. When you're knee-deep in it, "this too shall pass" can feel more like a cruel joke than a comforting mantra—especially when you have a heightened sensitivity to stress, like living with anxiety disorder. (At this point, I'm tempted to add "professional stress juggler" to my resume.) But here's the deal—it's not about waiting for the chaos to end (because, let's be honest, life is an ongoing circus). It's about learning how to manage the madness, even while it's still spinning—acknowledging that for some, the spinning feels a bit faster and harder to stop.

A deep breath won't fix everything, but it might keep you from snapping at your kid. A granola bar won't solve your problems, but it can stop you from spiraling over something trivial. In extreme stress, my husband often quips, "Look out the window. Do you see the end of the world? No? Exactly. We're going to survive this." It's a reminder to shift focus, no matter what storm we face.

That's the real victory: navigating the situation with your sanity (mostly) intact, knowing that managing the madness is less about perfection and more about persistence.

#shortyellowpencilRX—Your Daily Dose

Think about the last time stress made you snap at someone you care about. What was your body trying to tell you that you ignored? Clenched jaw? Racing heart? Aching stomach? Next time, what could you do to catch yourself before the explosion?

PAGE TURNER

So, you've now tried managing your stress with snacks, water, and the occasional time-out to no avail. It's time to jump into the ice bath of bad advice from *MADtv's* Dr. Switzer (more on him in a moment), who will kindly bury you alive in a box if you don't "Stop it." By the end of the next chapter, I'm pretty sure you'll be schooled to open your own "Dr. Switzer" practice. So grab your pencil and notepad because there will be a test.

I'm Not Here to Shish-ka-bob You

But Accidents "Do Happen"

Chapter 12

Stop It
(or I'll Bury You Alive in a Box!)

There's a classic *MADtv* sketch where Bob Newhart plays a therapist, "Dr. Switzer," whose hilariously simplistic approach to solving his clients' problems boils down to two words: "Stop it!" (If you haven't seen it, trust me, it's worth a quick YouTube search.) In the sketch, a woman nervously shares her fear of being buried alive in a box. Dr. Switzer listens patiently for two minutes before delivering his grand therapeutic advice: "Stop it." No matter the issue—whether it's trauma, compulsive behaviors, or irrational fears—his sessions always end with the same two-word solution. And his final threat to the client when she says his therapy isn't working? "Stop it, or I'll bury you alive in a box!"

It's absurd. It's heartless. And honestly, it's kind of hilarious. But here's the thing: who hasn't been tempted to offer that two-word advice? "Stop worrying." "Stop overthinking." "Stop spiraling." If only it were that simple, right? But let's be honest— if "stop it" worked, I wouldn't be writing this chapter, and you wouldn't be reading it. (By the way, get ready to dive into about 3,000 words here.)

The Real-Life Dr. Switzers

I've had my share of real-life "Dr. Switzers" (no medical training needed). You know the type: the ones who hear your very real worries and respond with things like, "It's all in your head," or "Just stop thinking about it." While their advice might technically hold some truth, the delivery? It's about as helpful as yelling "calm down" to someone on fire. Worry doesn't respond to commands. In fact, hearing those words often just adds fuel to the burn.

Take COVID, for example. Remember those endless months of quarantine when we were all trying to keep it together? For me, it wasn't just the isolation—the endless mask debates, the fear of germs, and the worry that seemed to latch onto everything. Germs felt like they were flying through the air like confetti, and every sneeze or cough became, to me, a potential catastrophe.

At one point, I was nursing a three-week migraine and absolutely terrified of going to the ER. Why? Because the virus had already taken the lives of some of my family and friends, and my brain was convinced that walking into a hospital—even triple-masked and gloved—was the same as willingly jumping into a pit of germs. The fear of catching something worse paralyzed me.

But I decided I needed to go. And there I was, driving to the ER, crying uncontrollably, and calling anyone who might help me find a sense of calm—my husband, my sister, even my boss. Worry had completely taken over, shining its relentless spotlight on every worst-case scenario. I couldn't think rationally.

I couldn't see past the overwhelming fear. I had boxed myself in, buried by my spiraling thoughts.

I got there first, but when my husband got to the ER, I could hear my heart pounding in my ears. With every passing minute, my anxiety grew, fueled by each spluttering cough and the sight of low-riding masks I witnessed in the waiting room. When I think about that time, my heart still hits the panic button.

Why "Stop It" Is Like Telling a Tornado to Chill

In such times, it becomes painfully clear why the Dr. Switzer method falls short. Worry doesn't politely knock on the door and wait for you to address it. It barges in, rearranges your priorities, and takes center stage in your mind. It plants itself so firmly that you're already trapped by the time you notice.

"Stop it" doesn't work because worry is persistent and sneaky. It convinces you it's doing you a favor—pointing out every possible danger so you can "prepare." But in reality, it's just spinning you in circles. And the more you try to fight it with blunt denial, the stronger it grows.

The real question isn't just how to get out of that box—it's how to stop crawling in there in the first place. Escaping the grip of worry takes more than a two-word command. It requires awareness, intentionality, and practical tools to address what's really going on.

In the following sections, we'll explore how to recognize the patterns of worry, reframe your thoughts, and take meaningful action to break free. While "Stop it" might not work, there is a way to regain control before worry buries you alive.

Worry vs. Anxiety: The Caffeinated Cousins

Before we go any further, let's clear something up: worry and anxiety are not the same thing—they're more like cousins who show up uninvited—but they bring very different baggage.

Worry is specific. It's tied to something real and often concrete. Think about that looming deadline, the weird noise your car is making, or whether you left the oven on. Worry is your brain trying to solve a problem or predict an outcome. It's annoying and persistent, but it stays mostly in your head.

Anxiety, on the other hand, is like worry's overachieving cousin. It doesn't stick to one problem; it casts a wide net of fear and unease. Anxiety doesn't just occupy your thoughts—it invades your body. Your heart races, your stomach churns, and your chest feels like it's being squeezed. It's not just about solving a problem; it's about feeling overwhelmed.

Worry taps you on the shoulder with specific concerns and shines them in your brain like a spotlight; anxiety is a group of caffeinated squirrels, each grabbing a mic and singing a different song on your stage—all at once.

Why Does It Matter?

Knowing the difference is essential because they require different approaches:

Worry often responds to action. If you're worried about something specific, like forgetting to pay a bill, taking a small step to fix the problem—like setting a reminder or paying it immediately—can ease your mind.

Anxiety isn't so easily handled. It often sticks around, even without a clear solution or problem. It requires grounding techniques, rest, and sometimes professional help to calm the storm.

Most of this chapter focuses on worry—that everyday mental nagging that keeps you from peace. But we can't ignore the fact that, if left unchecked, worry and day-to-day stress can multiply into those loosey-goosey, all-over-the-place unsettling feelings of anxiety—where your body starts firing on impulse alone. It's like someone just dumped a packet of pop rocks into your bloodstream. That's why recognizing the difference between worry and anxiety gives you a better battle plan to wrangle it before it takes over. What starts as a minor concern—"What if this goes wrong?"—snowballs into physical symptoms: a racing heart, stomach knots, and chest tightness.

sticky note to self

Worry is like dragging an elephant; anxiety is like dragging five elephants while getting zapped with live wires.

Meanwhile, your mind replays every mistake, every "what if," every fear. Worry doesn't care if the thought is logical; it spins the mental hamster wheel, leaving you exhausted.

I'm over half a century old, and I still catch myself fretting over a "0" I got in high school algebra. Does it matter now? Not even a little.

But worry thrives on repetition, wearing you down with every turn. You're rehearsing arguments with people who aren't even in the room. You know the ones—the shower arguments, the 2 AM spirals, the ones where you formulate your entire comeback before you've even talked to the person.

Recognizing when worry shifts from helpful problem-solving to paralyzing fear is key to stopping the spiral. Once worry starts to control your thoughts and actions instead of pointing you toward solutions, it's time to take back the mic.

When Panic Feels Like Your Favorite Fuzzy Socks

What's the most obnoxious thing about worry? Sometimes, people get used to living in "a worried state of being" for so long that it just feels safe. It's familiar. It becomes the mental bubble wrap we use to brace ourselves against the unknown. We convince ourselves we'll be prepared for anything if we consider every possible scenario.

However, there's a catch: while worry might feel productive, it's keeping you stuck. It tricks you into thinking you're in control, but in reality, it's just a safety net that doubles as a chain. Letting go of that chain isn't just uncomfortable—it's downright awkward. But it's the only way to stop living in survival mode.

Change Feels Just, Well, Awkward

Recognizing that you've grown comfortable with worry is hard. It's like trying to get up from a couch you've sunk into for years. Even though you know it's lumpy and terrible for your back, switching to a new seat feels awkward. Change feels vulnerable. What if life without worry feels worse?

This is the trap worry sets for us: it convinces us that letting go of it will leave us unprepared, unprotected, and out of control. But the truth is, holding onto worry keeps us from living fully. We can begin to break free when we stop seeing worry as a safety net and start recognizing it as a chain.

So How Do You Know You're Running a Worry Subscription Service?

Here are a few questions to ask yourself:

Does worry feel like second nature? If worrying feels automatic—like your go-to way of thinking—it's time to pause and evaluate.

Do you feel weird without it? When life is calm, do you search for something to worry about?

Is it affecting your relationships? Are your worries causing you to withdraw, lash out, or place unfair expectations on the people around you?

Is it stealing your peace? When was the last time you felt relaxed—like your mind wasn't spinning with all the "what ifs"?

Do you rename (or excuse) worry as "concern" or "care"? Maybe you're not really worried—you care deeply about something. (Sound familiar?)

If you don't worry, who will? Are your prayers anxious or peaceful? Maybe God doesn't need to be reminded—He's already covered it.

Rebooting Your Brain: The Ctrl+Alt+Delete of Mental Health

The great thing about our brains is that they're adaptable. Even if you've spent years letting worry run the show, it's not too late to change the pattern. But it starts with a choice: the choice to get uncomfortable for a while as you learn a new way of thinking. And yes, that new way of thinking might involve working with a counselor, psychiatrist, or even medication to help get you on the right track.

Here's what I've learned: It's awkward to stop worrying because worry gives us the illusion of control. But releasing worry doesn't mean losing control—it's admitting you never had control of something to begin with.

The Three-Ring Circus of Worry: Unicorns, Car Trouble, Death & Taxes

Regarding worry, I've found that most anxious thoughts fall into three categories: the irrational, the probable, and the inevitable. Each one requires a different approach to overcome.

1. The Irrational: "You're Going to Be Shish-ka-bobed by a Unicorn" Worries

Irrational worry is like a runaway train—entirely off the rails and heading somewhere absurd. It takes a tiny, often harmless concern, adds a truckload of drama, and transforms it into a full-blown epic catastrophe. You know it's not logical, but it still feels real.

Imagine this: you're lying awake at 2:00 a.m. Instead of focusing on sleep, your brain decides to replay that embarrassing thing you said in a podcast six months ago (this is my truth) or convince you to contemplate an utterly irrational disaster scenario—like being shish-ka-bobed by a unicorn—is waiting around the corner. Sure, it's ridiculous, but it doesn't matter now. It feels just as terrifying as something possible.

The truth about irrational worry is that it doesn't need facts to thrive. It only requires your imagination. And your imagination? Oh, it's a powerful storyteller.

When Your Brain Makes Your Body Believe Its Wild Stories

One of my daughters has a condition called somatic disorder, where her brain is so powerful that it can convince her body it's sick. As a baby, she could spike a fever purely from stress—no infection, no virus—just her mind sending signals that something was wrong.

As a teenager, the stress of school became so overwhelming that she'd throw up every morning on the way out the door.

Now, as an adult, she can read the side effects on a medication label and convince herself she's experiencing them. Her body reacts as if these imagined symptoms are real because, to her mind, they are real.

On top of this, she faces what I call "Cry Wolf Syndrome." She's constantly worried that people who know about her condition will dismiss her health concerns with a casual, "Oh, it's just stress."

That kind of dismissal stings. It makes her second-guess herself, amplifying her anxiety and leaving her questioning whether she's genuinely sick or if it's "just in her head."

It's a double-edged sword: her irrational worries create real physical symptoms, but the fear of being invalidated deepens her anxiety. This traps her in a frustrating cycle of fear and doubt—a cycle I know many people can relate to in their own ways.

2. The Probable: The Preemptive To-Do List

Probable worries feel heavier because they're rooted in reality. Could you lose your job? Yes. Could your car break down?

Absolutely. These aren't unicorn-level worries; they're real possibilities that could upend your plans.

The "I'm Just Being Prepared" Lie We Tell Ourselves

Here's the catch: probable worries like to pretend they're productive. Your brain says, "If I think about this enough, I'll find a solution." But instead of solving the problem, you're stuck running in mental circles. It's like mopping the floor while the faucet is still running—your energy is spent, but the worry remains. For example:

You hear a weird noise from your car. Instead of calling a mechanic, you spend hours Googling every possible cause, from a loose muffler to a sudden sinkhole waiting to swallow your vehicle whole.

You're worried about an upcoming meeting. Instead of preparing what you'll say, you replay every worst-case scenario until you're convinced it will end in disaster.

Probable worries can quickly take over because they feel so valid. After all, they could happen. Instead of helping you prepare, they often leave you exhausted before you've taken a single step.

The Snowball Effect:
From Small Worry to Full-Blown Avalanche

The danger with probable worries is their tendency to spiral. What starts as a single concern—like, "What if I can't pay the bills next month?"—snowballs into fears about losing your home, stability, and sense of control.

They sneak in, wearing the mask of logic. But instead of guiding you to action, they trap you in a never-ending game of mental "what if." The more you dwell on them, the more they expand into harder-to-manage territory.

3. The Inevitable: When You Can't Avoid It

Some worries are not just possible—they're guaranteed. Aging parents, grief, change, and world events are realities no one can control or escape. In the face of these certainties, these worries can still feel overwhelming, weighing on your mind and heart like an anchor you can't lift. Without a deeper sense of faith, they can feel even heavier, taking up permanent residence in your thoughts. They replay fears of loss, uncertainty, and that constant, nagging question: What if I can't handle this?

Here's what I've learned: while you can't stop these things from happening, you can choose how to respond. For me, it's about surrendering the weight of the inevitable to someone strong enough to carry it. However, no matter where you land in faith, we all have a choice. We can let worry take over, consuming our thoughts and energy, or we can face the inevitable with courage, perspective, and hope. While challenges may be unavoidable, they don't have to ruin every day of life or steal our peace.

Surrender: The Strongest Move in Your Mental Chess Game

Surrender doesn't mean ignoring your problems. It means recognizing the things draining your well-being—the ones you can't change and those you were never meant to handle alone. It's not about giving up; it's about releasing the weight of trying to control everything.

Instead, focus on what you can practically do today—what is within your power. Be honest with yourself (and others) about the things you can't do, and permit yourself to let those go. Some battles aren't yours to fight, and some outcomes aren't yours to control—and that's okay.

Reality will always bring challenges, but surrender reminds you this is not your battle to win. It grounds you in the peace that comes from knowing you're not in charge of every outcome—and that's okay.

How to Unplug the Worry Machine Before It Overheats

Whether your worry is irrational, probable, or inevitable, you can take steps to loosen its grip. The good news? Worry doesn't have to run the show. Here's how to regain control:

Name It—Write down what's bothering you. Naming it brings clarity and often shrinks its size. Seeing it in black and white gives you a starting point. For me, it can involve opening my Bible and reflecting on certain verses. Journaling or coloring while focusing on making art projects from words of truth and encouragement is a productive way to calm my mind and hands.

Reality Check It—Ask yourself: Is this thought based on facts or assumptions? Replace fear-driven guesses with what you know to be true. For example, if you're worried about a meeting, write down what you actually know about it—what's been said or planned—instead of spiraling into imagined worst-case scenarios. Truth has a way of shrinking fear.

sticky note to self

Life is full of "What Ifs," but heaven is in control of the "Even Ifs."

Ask: What Can I Control?—Focus on the part you can control, no matter how small. For example, are you worried about your car breaking down? Schedule a mechanic checkup. Practice with a friend or jot down key points if you need a presentation. Finances? Review your budget or brainstorm small ways to save. Taking one intentional step cuts through worry's paralysis and reminds you that you're not powerless.

Take Action —Then Stop: Do what's within your control, and then stop. Overthinking or over-preparing won't change the outcome—it'll just drain you. Let your action be enough, and choose to let go of the rest.

Say NOPE—When a worry starts to spiral, interrupt it by saying, "NOPE." Say it firmly, out loud if you have to. Your brain doesn't have to follow every path your thoughts wander down. Saying "NOPE" disrupts the cycle and gives you back control over your mental narrative.

Watch What You're Feeding Your Mind—Your brain is a sponge, soaking up whatever you pour into it. Doomscrolling, overexposure to negative news, or consuming anxiety-inducing entertainment amplifies worry. Limit those inputs and intentionally replace them with things that uplift and encourage. Philippians 4:8 is a perfect guide: "Whatever is true, whatever is noble, whatever is right, whatever is pure … think about such things" (NIV).

Ground Yourself in the Present—Use your senses to anchor yourself to the present. Ask: What can I see, hear, or feel right now? Grounding techniques—like holding a comforting object, listening to soothing sounds, or physically connecting with someone through a hug or handhold—can calm your nervous system and interrupt the spiral.

The Frantic Text Tornado: "CALL ME NOW!"

If there's one thing I've perfected when worry hits, it's my "call me now" reflex. The second my brain detects even the faintest whiff of trouble, I reach for my phone, firing off a rapid succession of texts: "Call me now. Call me now. Call me right now!"

> If it's been more than one minute without a reply—I start texting in ALL CAPS.

It doesn't matter what they're doing—whether it's in the middle of a staff training session, taking a break to use the loo, or operating a chainsaw—I'm convinced my worry should stop the world from spinning. Do that "hold it in" dance a little bit longer, drop the saw, and solve my problem immediately! My poor husband and kids have probably grown to dread those words.

Does this sound familiar? Maybe you've done the same— spamming someone with texts or voicemails that scream urgency. You're overwhelmed, panicked, and convinced you'd finally find peace if someone else could answer or fix it. The irony, of course, is that this knee-jerk reaction rarely fixes anything. Instead, it drags others into our whirlwind, leaving everyone more stressed and frazzled.

Swapping Emergency Calls for Heavenly Help

But what if we took that same urgency and redirected it? Instead of spamming loved ones with "Call me now!" texts, what if we tried something different?

Whether your worry is irrational (like the fear of a unicorn ambush), probable (like a car making a weird noise), or inevitable (like grief or change), the solution isn't frantic texts or external fixes. For me, it's about pausing, redirecting the panic, and shifting to prayer.

This reframing just makes my whole body find the fullness of oxygen. Instead of drowning my family in my spiral, I've learned to take that panic—the tightness in my chest, the frantic racing of my thoughts—and turn it into a prayer: "Calm me now. Calm me now."

It's not about having the perfect words or fixing the problem instantly. It's about finding peace in the midst of panic mode.

If prayer isn't your thing, find your own way to redirect that energy—whether through deep breathing, redirecting your focus to a tree or a pretty picture, or simply speaking calming words to yourself. The point is to interrupt the frantic "fix it now" cycle with something that brings you back to center.

Trading Your Panic Room for a Viewing Deck

This shift—from "call me now" to "calm me now"—isn't just about finding temporary peace. It's about opening yourself to the possibility that maybe, just maybe, the thing you're so worried about isn't as hopeless as it seems.

What if, instead of spiraling into "What if everything goes wrong?" we started asking, "What if something good comes out of this?"

What if that irrational worry pushes us to grow? What if the probable fear teaches us something valuable? What if the inevitable leads to a deeper understanding or a new direction?

#shortyellowpencilRX—Your Daily Dose

Think about a time when worry kept you from doing something you really wanted to do. How did that experience shape your decisions afterward? If you could go back and give yourself some advice, what would you say?

PAGE TURNER 

If worry is the sugared-up chipmunks singing in your brain, tiredness is the sloth that's eaten all your motivation and then fallen asleep holding it hostage. Let's journey to the world of "Tired Has Crept Up All Into My Bones"—where you're not just fighting the urge to worry about everything, you're fighting the urge to care about anything. On second thought, maybe we can all just roll over and hope we hit the next page.

RANDOM DOODLE SPACE

May the Overthinking Octopus
of Your Life

Reserve the Right to be Silent

Chapter 13

Tired Has Crept Up All Into My Bones
(And Brought All Its Luggage)

"I get so used to living for the week to be over … for seasons to be over … for stages of life to be more of what I can manage … for the next item that needs to be changed … if I could only get to the place of somewhere down the road. Am I thinking life will get closer to easy when I get closer to old? Counting down the days before I get there to find that they've already passed and I'm wishing life could find stillness in the weeks I wished wouldn't last …"

I remember writing this when I could barely get out of bed in the thick of my mental health breakdown, but to be honest, I feel like this battle with weariness has been more than fifty years long—and everyday it's a battle.

When Tiredness Holds Your Remote Control

Weariness has a way of hijacking our sensibilities and shifting our settings to autopilot. It's not just about being tired—though those sleepless nights where you've counted enough sheep to start your wool factory don't help. That soul-deep exhaustion settles into our bones and becomes the lead weight in our days, thoughts, and emotions. Everything just feels heavier. Tiredness holds the remote control of your life and keeps mindlessly flipping the channels of your day. You wake up tired, going through the motions, wondering where your strength went and how you ended up at work without remembering you were driving the car.

Beware of The Octopus of Overthinking

Ever notice how weariness and overthinking are besties who enable each other's worst habits? It's like they've signed a pact: "I'll make you too tired to think clearly, and you'll spend what little energy you have obsessing over things you can't control." It's the world's worst partnership, and you're somehow the unwilling business manager.

My brain turns into an overthinking octopus—and much like this fascinating creature, each tentacle of thought has its own anxious little brain, all firing simultaneously. The cruel irony is that when you're at your most depleted, your brain works overtime on the exact thoughts that drain you further. It's like having an accountant who keeps embezzling from your already-empty bank account.

Sticky note to self

Your overthinking brain is like an overprotective parent with terrible judgment.

When I'm exhausted, my brain likes to host late-night worry parties where only catastrophic thoughts are invited. That minor comment my friend made three weeks ago? Let's dissect it at 2:00 a.m.! That email I sent with a typo? Clearly career-ending! The way my neighbor looked at me while I was bringing in groceries? They must be plotting something sinister involving my recycling bin!

My personal overthinking specialties include:

Replaying conversations I had five years ago and coming up with better responses now

Convincing myself that silence from someone means they hate me (rather than, you know, they're busy living their lives)

Remembering I turned in a design job to a client without correcting what they requested

Planning detailed responses to arguments that haven't happened yet and probably never will

The recurring nightmare about the "D" I made in Algebra II in 12th grade—and having to go back to school to retake the class (no lie, almost thirty-five years later and I still stress about it appearing on my transcript)

The Overthinking Escape Hatch

Breaking free from the overthinking spiral takes more than just telling yourself to "stop thinking about it" (which is about as effective as telling a toddler to calm down). Here's what actually helps me cut the power to my mental hamster wheel:

The Thought Parking Lot—Keep a small notebook by your bed. When overthinking strikes at night, write down the thought and say to yourself, "I've parked this thought. I have permission to pick it up tomorrow when I'm rested." Sometimes, just the act of "setting it down" somewhere gives your brain permission to let go.

The Physical Interrupt—Sometimes, you need to physically jolt your brain out of its loop. I splash cold water on my face, turn on music and sing, or even do jumping jacks. Changing your physical state can reset your mental state. Remember: your tired brain is preschooler with a power tool—it means well, but causes destruction without proper supervision.

When Your Brain.exe Has Stopped Working

When weariness takes over, your mind bears the brunt. Decision-making becomes nearly impossible. Suddenly, choosing what to eat for dinner feels like you're trying to solve quantum physics. "Cereal or sandwich?" becomes an existential crisis that could rival any philosophy dissertation.

Your concentration scatters (hello, reading the same paragraph seventeen times), memory falters ("Why did I walk into this room again?"), and creative thinking shuts down faster than a laptop with 1% battery.

> That mental fog isn't laziness,
> it's your brain sending out an SOS.

The worst part? Your internal dialogue turns into that catty commentator nobody asked for. The voice that once encouraged now criticizes: "Why can't you keep up? Everyone else manages just fine.

Karen over there is running a marathon while raising triplets and writing her third novel, and you can barely remember to put on matching socks." Negative thoughts grow louder while perspective shrinks faster than a cotton sweater in a hot dryer.

Your Body's Subscription to "Aches Monthly" Just Auto-Renewed

When weariness sets in, let me tell you, it's not a generous scorekeeper. The headaches, the muscle tension that makes you walk like you're auditioning for *The Walking Dead*, the compromised immune system—these aren't coincidences. When I'm at my weariest, my body raises more white flags than a surrender convention: digestive issues flare up, sleep becomes either impossible or the only thing I want (usually at the most inappropriate times, like during important Zoom calls), and my energy reserve hits zero even before I've elasticized my uncombed hair into messy-bun mode—it's not just a hairstyle, it's a way of life.

This physical exhaustion creates a vicious cycle worthy of a villainous monologue. You're too tired to exercise, but your energy drops further without movement. You reach for quick energy fixes—sugar, caffeine, those energy drinks that taste like liquefied electricity— anything to push through, which only sets you up for deeper crashes later. It's like borrowing energy from tomorrow, except tomorrow comes with interest rates that would make a loan shark blush.

Operation Sanity to the Rescue

Fighting weariness requires a multifaceted approach—to simultaneously address mind, body, and spirit. Here are strategies that have helped me (when I actually remember to use them—which, let's be honest, is about as consistent as my attempts to fold fitted sheets):

Body Rescues for the Too-Tired-to-Move Club

The Laziest Workout Plan Ever—Too tired for a workout? Try a five-minute stretch or gentle walk. Small movement beats no movement. Dancing to one song in your kitchen counts. Chasing the dog who stole your sock definitely counts.

The Permission Slip for Grown-Ups—Schedule ten-minute power breaks throughout your day instead of pushing through. Set an alarm and actually take them, even if all you do is stare blankly into space. Sometimes, that's exactly what your brain needs.

Not Just Another Water Lecture—Dehydration mimics fatigue. And quick carbs lead to crashes—pair them with protein for steadier energy. Yes, this means your body needs actual water, not the juice you just squeezed out of that cherry Life Saver.

Hug Therapy (No Co-Pay Required)—Never underestimate the power of a hug, a weighted blanket, or self-massage to reset your nervous system. In a pinch, petting a dog works wonders (cats work, too, but on their mysterious schedule).

Spirit Boosters That Don't Require a Personality Transplant

The Joy Scavenger Hunt—Keep a list of small things that bring you life—the cranberry orange aroma wafting from your wax warmer, watching water ripple across the pond (sometimes during a sunrise walk round the pond, I've seen those ripples flow in the opposite direction to the drop off and it mesmerizes me)—and deliberately seek one each day. Mine include watching people fumble around in produce boxes to seize the perfect avocado.

The No-Performance Zone—Find spaces where you can just

Sticky note to self

Give much.
Expect nothing.
That's when life
will tap you on
the shoulder.

be—whether in prayer, with trusted friends, or in nature—without needing to perform. No jazz hands required.

Hope Borrowing (Better Interest Rates Than the Bank)—When you can't find your own, lean on someone else's until yours returns. Read inspiring stories. Call your most hopeful friend (you know, the one who's annoying when you're in a bad mood, but exactly who you need right now).

Pull-Over-And-Ask-For-Directions—When weariness takes the wheel, it's easy to think the solution is to push harder. But what if the real answer is to pull over and acknowledge what we need? For me, that means leaning into my faith. But even if that's not your path, the principle remains: sometimes strength comes from admitting we can't do it all alone. Shocking, I know.

The "Choose Your Own Adventure" Rest Method

Some find peace in meditation, others in therapy, still others in prayer. I've found my anchor in faith, but I've seen friends find their rest in other ways:

Mindfulness practices (which I first misheard as "mindlessness practices" and thought, "I'm already pretty good at that")

Support groups

Professional counseling

Creative expression

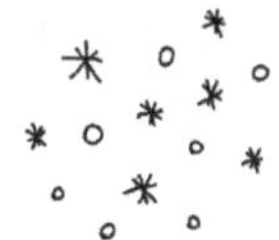

Deep connections with others

Time in nature

Simple stillness

The Plastic Houseplant Theory of Recovery

Remember all the plastic plants I have in pots in my garden I talked about a few chapters ago? They are faking it, they have no photosynthesis power to give life back to the world around them. They can just sit there and be looked at. (They do look so hearty in the snow.) Recovery from weariness isn't about dramatic changes but gentle, consistent care. Your spirit needs actual nourishment, not just the appearance of life.

Don't wait until you have the energy for a complete life overhaul. Start where you are. One glass of water. One deep breath. One moment of connection. One truth to counter the lies. Your weariness didn't appear overnight, and it won't disappear that way, either. But each day, you have to make the small choice to take care of your mind, body, and spirit, which is a step toward restoration—even when you can't feel the difference yet.

The One-Inch Journey Award Ceremony

If you're feeling weary today and wondering how to keep going, remember this: you're not alone in this struggle. Whether you find strength in faith, friendship, or resilience, your exhaustion is valid, and your journey matters. Sometimes victory looks like simply making it through another day without calling your boss a nincompoop or setting fire to your to-do list.

Wherever you are in your tired, I hope you'll find comfort in knowing that this weariness doesn't define you. It's not a character flaw or a failure—it's part of being human.

Tiredness also doesn't have a wham-bam solution. There will be setbacks. Days when the fog feels thicker. Those times when you wonder if you're moving backward. That's normal. Keep going. Keep trying. The smallest step counts, especially on the hardest days. And hey, if today all you did was survive without yelling at a stranger, I'm counting that as a win.

#shortyellowpencilRX—Your Daily Dose

Remember a time when weariness revealed a strength in you that surprise-visited like an old friend you'd forgotten you had. How did that bone-deep exhaustion eventually lead you to unexpected clarity or connection?

PAGE TURNER

Now, if you'll excuse me, I think we all deserve a twenty-minute nap before we continue. Because without proper rest, my brain switches to what I call Hobbit mode (let me curl in an underground house and hibernate for the next six months.)

RANDOM DOODLE SPACE

The Ministry of Silly Walks

(The Neurosparkly Brain's
Gift to the World)

Currently Closed

for Internal Processing.

Chapter 14

My Life as a Hole-Dwelling Extrovert
(A Guide to Embracing Relationships
and Finding Rest)

I love people. Like, I REALLY love people—the way my dogs love peanut butter, except I don't lick the furniture afterward. I love making them laugh until they snort-giggle (a personal victory that should come with a trophy), reminding them of their worth when they've forgotten, and encouraging them to embrace who they were truly made to be. And yet, if you've ever known the bittersweet truth of giving too much of yourself, you know that loving people can be as draining as it is uplifting.

Sometimes, I feel like Cinderella—except in my version, it's not a fairy godmother who swoops in with a glittering gown. It's me at 10:00 p.m., collapsed on my office couch, emotionally bankrupt, wondering if binge-watching Just Being Melanie's *We Do Not Care Club* shorts counts as "spiritual rest." Every request, every conversation, and every act of compassion leaves me feeling like I've been put through an emotional spin cycle. Because honestly, everything—even good things—requires energy. I have to decompress.

So buckle up, Buttercup! I invite you into my half-hermit, half-hobbit existence as I reveal what I've learned. Because I reach a point where juggling my love for people and my need for solitude feels less like a delicate balance and more like trying to put skinny jeans on after Thanksgiving dinner—and it's taking a toll on my mental health faster than I can say, "Where's my comfort blanket?"

"The "I Love You, Now Please Go Away" Paradox"

Here's the thing nobody tells you: even joyful interactions drain my social battery. After an interview, a consultation, or even coffee with a friend I adore, I need what I call "recovery time." It's not gradual—it's immediate. One moment I'm fully present and engaged, the next I'm horizontal wondering if words are still required. This isn't the general exhaustion from Chapter 13—this is specifically social depletion. My neurodivergent brain manually operates every social gear while others coast on autopilot. When it's over, I need silence, solitude, and snacks. Non-negotiable.

I'm a social hermit—a hobbit who occasionally throws spectacular parties, then needs three days to recover in my hole with a "Do Not Disturb" sign. I thrive on deep, one-on-one conversations where vulnerability meets humor, but crowds? That's like running a marathon in platform heels while someone follows you with a tambourine.

sticky note to self

My soft heart was made to live behind bars for its own protection.

I pour every drop of energy into making others feel seen, only to find myself completely drained afterward, staring into my refrigerator at midnight wondering if cheese and crackers counts as a balanced dinner (it does if there's a grape on the plate, right?).

Even when I'm in my element—cracking jokes or offering wisdom like "you can't pour from an empty cup"—ironically, I'm handing out ice cubes and good intentions. That's why I'm learning that needing to recharge isn't antisocial—it's the only mode of survival.

The Blessing and Curse of a Heart that Feels Deeply

Let's get real honest about something here. Most of us are freely handing out keys to our emotional apartments like we're running an Airbnb. We're letting everyone and their cousin's opinion set up camp in our head space, and then we wonder why we're exhausted. This is because empathy is a double-edged sword.

Honestly? It's one of the greatest gifts I've been given—being able to feel what other people feel. That's where real connection happens. When a friend is hurting, I carry that hurt with them. When someone is anxious, I pick up on their worry like a second skin. It's a deep, abiding connection that has the power to heal—but also the potential to break me if I'm not careful.

The Art of Saying "No" Without Adding "Sorry" a Trillion Times

My friend Lisa says I'd dish myself out to everyone in spoonfuls if I could—serving up "Amber soup" until all that's left is an empty ladle. One of the hardest lessons I've learned is where to draw the line before I cross it, trailing my sanity behind me like toilet paper stuck to a shoe.

Here's what I've learned about saying no without the guilt:

Just say it plainly. "I can't" is a complete sentence. You don't need a three-paragraph explanation about your schedule, your energy levels, and your third cousin's dental appointment.

Stop apologizing for having limits. Saying "I'm sorry, but…" makes it sound like you're doing something wrong by protecting your peace. You're not. Try "I'm not able to" instead of "I'm so sorry but maybe I could…"

My Sanity-Saving Toolkit

Over time, I've developed some tools for protecting my energy and preserving my joy. These aren't just platitudes; they're practical, hard-won lessons learned from the trenches of emotional exhaustion and spiritual burnout. Here are two of the most critical in my relationships with people, because they steal the most peace from my life.

Don't Seek Out Approval— It's tempting to think you're in a never-ending popularity contest where the prize is … more exhaustion? If I spent all my social energy trying to make everyone like me, I'd have the personality of a bland rice cake and the energy of a sloth on vacation. We don't have to take on the role of a one-person entertainment committee with jazz hands permanently attached. Sometimes, just showing up authentically—bedhead, bleach stains, and all—is more than enough.

Refuse to Collect Offenses—My friend Jackie shared this truth that has stuck with me: In a world brimming with drama more entertaining than reality TV, when you feel tension building over someone's offhand remark, pause, take a deep breath, and let it slide right off like water on a duck's back. People are going to tick you off more regularly than a metronome with a caffeine addiction, but stewing about it only hurts you while they post vacation photos having forgotten the whole thing. Forgiveness is the ultimate act of self-care and saves you storage space since grudges take up a lot of emotional real estate.

Finding Sacred Space in a World That Never Stops Buzzing (Or Texting, Or Emailing, Or Demanding...)

In a world that practically demands we perform social acrobatics 24/7, carving out sacred, solitary space can feel like trying to find Tinker Bell in Times Square—during New Year's Eve—while wearing a blindfold.

Relationships are more precious than ever—we learned that during the pandemic when every laugh and shared snippet of existence felt like a lifeline tossed into our isolation bubbles. Yet, amidst the constant invitations, pings, and check-ins, there comes a point where even the thought of venturing into public spaces makes you want to retreat into your own cozy fortress of solitude.

Here's the balancing act: relationships are the gourmet feast that enriches our souls, but self-care is that essential soak in a warm tub (and prevents us from saying things we'll have to apologize for later). When you take time for yourself, you're not abandoning the world; you're releasing yourself from the tangles of life so you can actually enjoy meaningful connection.

So, if part of you longs for a quiet nook instead of the roar of a crowd-filled food court, embrace it. Put down the phone, turn off the notifications, and breathe like it's going out of style. After all, even the most vibrant social butterfly needs to cocoon every now and then—if only to change into a fresh pair of wings or better yet, fresh from the dryer yoga pants.

Laughs, Limits, and Lessons for Life

I have times where I'm so peopled-out, I accidentally put my friends on radio silence for months without realizing it. But planned get-togethers—even though they require recovery time—also remind me what I'm missing. Like impromptu van chats with my bestie Tabatha, or walks at the park with Philip where we share the chaotic mess of our lives and laugh at life's absurdity. By the end of those times, it's like someone hit the reset button on my soul.

My extroverted introvert heart is resilient because it knows when to reach out and when to retreat.

Philip is my comedic counterpart—our walks at the park provide the laughter and fresh air my head desperately needs. Those shared moments aren't just a distraction from the deadlines of life—they're a celebration of life's beautiful absurdity. It's the reminder that even when the world seems intent on wearing you down, there's always a spark that pulls a smile to your face.

You Don't Have to Pull Everyone Close

Loving others means accepting them just as they are—even when their quirks and flaws make you shake your head. But your energy is a precious resource. You don't have to pull everyone close to feel connected or to validate your capacity for love.

Keep laughing, keep loving, and give yourself permission to stay whole. You can't give yourself away in pieces and expect to survive. But complete isolation isn't the answer either. The magic is in knowing who gets the front-row seat to your life— and being okay with the fact that not everyone makes the cut.

#shortyellowpencilRX—Your Daily Dose

Think about a time when your need for solitude clashed with someone else's desire for your company. How did you navigate that tension? What would you do differently now? Extra credit: What's one way you can protect your peace-even if it's just five minutes of quiet before someone asks where their socks are?

PAGE TURNER

PAGE TURNER 

So that's the life of a hole-dwelling extrovert—loving people from my cave, one carefully curated social interaction at a time, with adult Lunchables and Jane Austen as my emotional support system.

But what happens when you can't retreat to your cave because tiny humans need you 24/7? What happens when your need for silence crashes headlong into someone's need for ... well, everything? Enter the spicy life of neurodivergent parenting if you dare.

Seasoned with Love

Sprinkled in Chaos

#shortyellowpencilRXfunnies

Chapter 15

Neurospicy Parenting
(in a Great Expectations World)

If you thought managing your brain was complicated, wait until someone hands you little brains to take home that work like yours but are infused with their own unique glitches.

Welcome to neurospicy parenting, where nobody gets a cave, everyone's feelings are big, and most of the day is focused on just trying to make it to bedtime without losing our minds.

We all agree on one thing—even though Imogen (Immy) and Penelope (Pen) are young adults still at home, we're still working to master lessons in conflict resolution as well as mental interpretive dance. Some days we nail the choreography. Other days we crash into each other and call it character building.

That Mellow Yellow Girl (My Grand Plans for Her to Be Better Than Me—She IS, In Spite of Me)

I should have known after we named our oldest daughter Saffron (Saffy) after one of my favorite Donovan hits from the sixties, the extent of our parenting journey would be powdered with the most pricey and hardest to farm spices in existence. Harvested from the crocus flower, saffron requires painstaking labor—so much so that, ounce for ounce, it's more expensive than gold. Let me say that again—MORE EXPENSIVE THAN GOLD!

So, I'll never forget the day we were at Walmart, tallying up the cost of school clothes and supplies, when my kindergartener turned to me and said, "You shouldn't have named me after the most expensive spice in the world."

Little did I know how appropriate that name would be.

Saffy—and her two younger sisters, Immy, and Pen—turned out to be rare and precious in ways I never could have anticipated. They weren't just quirky because they had me as their mother. Each had their own unique neurodivergent challenges— challenges my husband and I initially (and spectacularly) failed to parent out of them.

Today, Saffy is 25, Immy is 22, and Pen is 18—graduating high school as this book goes to print. But this story starts years ago, when they were small and naturally, their Mum and Dad were clueless. (We own that now.)

Am I Really Qualified to Be in Charge?

We adults dealing with ADHD often think we should be better by now. That somehow, by the time we're parenting, we should have figured this out. But that's not the case.

What if you're not above your kids' struggles? What if you're right there in the trenches with them—just with twenty more years of coping mechanisms and a driver's license?

What if you're playing in the same playground as your kids? You just happen to be the responsible party.

I have to be honest—this can feel sharper for neurodivergent parents like me. We're already trying to adult the best way we know how, and we're handed these small lives and asked to teach skills we're still learning ourselves.

So we land in the Cactus Forest of Parenthood—wanting to be ourselves, while the world hints we're too old to still be figuring this out.

We show up as the prickly pear. Sweet. Vulnerable. And still part of the cacti family. Sure we belong—until we realize we don't have the thorns to match our name.

But we're not broken. We're just playing in the same park we're supposed to be supervising. And sometimes, that's the most honest kind of parenting there is.

My Multi-tasking is Someone Else's Kryptonite

For years, I parented from my own dysfunctional thinking, failing to see beyond it. Before I discovered we all had these hurdles, I expected my girls to function the way I did. I'd rattle off instructions like a drill sergeant on espresso:

"Grab your shoes! Pack your lunch! Did you brush your teeth? Change your clothes! Finish your homework! Feed the dogs! And we're leaving NOW!"

Then, one rainy morning, as I passed an umbrella to Immy, who just had her backpack in tow, she then froze mid-reach and snapped, "Mum, I can only hold one thing at a time!"

sticky note to self

In the unpredictable sport of parenting, improvisation wins the gold.

Her frustration was real and punched me in the chest. Immy wasn't defying me. While my ADHD thrives on juggling thirty-seven things at once, Immy needed to process the world one clear instruction at a time. I wasn't helping them succeed— and I was setting them up to feel like failures.

I Just Can't Get These Fish to Ride Bicycles

For years, I believed good parenting meant preparing my kids to navigate the real world. I thought if I just parented hard enough, I could mold them into strong, capable, independent adults. However, when Pen, had her first neuropsych evaluation, her psychiatrist dropped a truth bomb that rewired my thinking, "You can't grade a fish on how well it rides a bicycle."

That floored me.

For years, I had been holding my daughters to neurotypical standards, unknowingly setting them up to fail by asking them to navigate a world that wasn't built for them.

But what if the real challenge wasn't preparing them for the world—but preparing the world for them?

And the funny thing? I literally haven't been able to teach my girls to ride a bike.

Saffy managed, but Immy and Pen? Not a chance. Between balance issues and sheer terror, they wanted nothing to do with it. We tried, we wobbled, we fell, we called it a day. They still can't ride bikes, and that's okay.

More importantly, I had to rewire my own thinking—they didn't have to get straight "A"s, go to college, or force themselves to be outgoing to succeed.

Success isn't about meeting someone else's expectations. It's about my kids becoming exactly who they were made to be—on their own timeline, in their own way. Full stop.

When Labels Become Liberation

People love to complain that "everyone's putting a label on everything these days." I'm going to be really raw here—this is one statement that can make me go Mama Bear.

When Pen had her neuropsych exam and realized she was autistic, she said: "When I realized what I was dealing with, all of a sudden my mind made sense to me, and I didn't feel as bad about what I was struggling with."

THAT is what labels do. They're not limitations—they're explanations. They give you a checklist. They help you see: "Oh, these are common symptoms. I'm not broken. My brain just works differently."

Labels aren't the problem. Shame is the problem. Using labels to limit people is the problem. But understanding what's actually happening in your brain? That's not a label. That's a lighthouse.

Big Emotions, Small Hands, and the Judgment of Others

It took me years to stop apologizing for my kids' behavior and start celebrating their resilience. Their tears, quirks, and "different" ways of being aren't things to hide—they're parts of who they are.

Instead of justifying, I now advocate for their right to exist as they are.

Judgment from others isn't just frustrating—it's isolating. When you're parenting neurodivergent kids, it feels like there's a constant spotlight on you, magnifying every tear, every meltdown, and every quirk for public scrutiny. People love to throw their opinions at you, especially if you are a neurodivergent parent, because what you're thinking is naturally "off the tracks" of normality and you need help to parent correctly.

I've heard it all:

"Why does your child cry so much?"

"When I was a kid, my parents spanked ADHD out of me."

"Every kid does that. People just want excuses for everything now."

"Your kid wears the same three sets of clothes all the time—are you sure they're okay?"

"You should teach your kids to look people in the eyes when they talk."

Then come the deeper digs—the ones that cut straight through you:

sticky note to self

Love louder than the world criticizes.

"She's exaggerating or faking this."

"Is she still struggling?"

"You need to get her professional help—you're not qualified to handle this."

"Is this caused by social media?"

"I can't believe you're tolerating this. Make her____"

There are times when you feel like your kids' lives are full-blown community projects, and everyone thinks they should be involved in the planning meeting. The worst part? These comments don't just come from strangers—they come from the people who are supposed to love and support you.

The Silence That Hurts Most

But sometimes, it's not the comments that sting the most—it's the silence. It's the friends who slowly disappear, the families who pull away, the people who don't call or check in because you've become too much.

A close friend once told me, "The worst part isn't that they don't understand. It's that they don't want to understand." That comment was a mic drop to my head—that's exactly how it feels.

When you're in the trenches of parenting a child with complex needs, it's not just about meltdowns, doctor's appointments, or school meetings. It's realizing that some people will see your situation, decide it's too messy, and quietly wash their hands of you. Especially when you are parenting neurodivergent young adults with higher support needs.

And I get it—messiness is hard. Nobody wants to willingly dive into uncertainty.

But those who do? The ones who say, "I've got your back for however long this takes"? They are everything.

They're the ones who understand when:

Your adult daughters retreat to their bedrooms the moment anyone comes over—not because they're rude, but because the sensory and social overwhelm is too much. Even when it's your friend. Even when it's family.

It takes twelve years for your kid to stop wetting the bed, and by that time you're too tired to keep apologizing for the laundry pile.

Dinner plans fall apart because sensory overload hit, and you just can't.

Mostly, they remind you of this: You are not alone.

They're also the ones who:

Don't judge when you text at 2:00 a.m. because your brain won't shut off and you need someone to know you're still fighting.

Celebrate the micro-victories with you—like remembering to eat lunch or finding your keys on the first try.

Show up with sunflowers of understanding when you're too exhausted to explain why today was hard.

The Hardest Part about Judgment

The hardest part is that judgment comes from people who only see a sliver of the story.

They don't see:

The hours of research we've done to understand their needs.

The therapy, counseling, and advocacy battles we've fought behind closed doors.

The mental gymnastics we go through to anticipate their needs and help them navigate a world that wasn't built for them.

But the Sisterhood? We've seen it all. We've lived it. And we never ask you to justify why you're doing everything humanly possible to help your child thrive.

But they DO see my girls showing up every day—Saffy speaking at the state capitol for Disability Legislation Day, Immy managing screaming preschoolers despite sensory overload, or Pen ordering her own food when it terrifies her. That courage? It doesn't need explanation. It speaks for itself.

The composure it takes for Immy, who is easily overstimulated, to step into a classroom and help the teacher manage a room full of screaming babies or worse—preschoolers. (On her very first day she changed her first ever diaper, even with her sensory issues.)

The courage it takes for Pen to walk into a restaurant and order her own food—or the struggle to remember to turn in an assignment she already finished. Or all the end of term late nights she pulls to get those grades to passing.

These experiences? They're everything.

The Weight of Expectations

And it's not just strangers who pile on the judgment. Teachers expect kids to "grow out" of behaviors without offering the support they need to grow into themselves. Friends say, "Well, my kid never acts like that," with a hint of superiority. Even family members chime in with, "You just need to be firmer with her," as if the solution is as simple as flipping a switch.

The world looks at my young adult daughters and expects them to conform, to move faster to "just get over it." But neurodivergence doesn't come with an expiration date. It doesn't magically disappear when someone turns eighteen or twenty-one. My girls are navigating a world that wasn't built for them, and they're doing it with courage, resilience, and grace.

But as a neurodivergent mom, watching my kids with similar struggles face these impossible expectations is gut-wrenching.

Every critical comment aimed at them feels like a direct hit to me, reopening my own wounds from years of struggling with my mental health. I know what it feels like to be misunderstood, and I want to shield them from that. But I also know they need to learn how to stand on their own strength.

It's Not Extreme Makeover—Kids Edition

As a parent of now neurospicy young adults, my job has never been to make them more palatable to the world but to love them as they are and teach them to do the same.

That doesn't mean the judgment doesn't sting. It does. But instead of explaining or justifying, I let those comments roll off me (most of the time). I've learned that advocacy isn't about crafting the perfect explanation for why my young adult children are the way they are—it's about standing beside them, not in front of them, trying to make their differences more digestible for others.

For years, I acted as the Family Spokesperson, constantly clarifying, defending, and running interference. "Oh, she's not being rude; she's just overwhelmed." "She's not ignoring you; social anxiety makes small talk exhausting." But I'm learning to skip the PR campaign. My kids don't need me translating their existence. They are who they are, and that's enough.

So now, instead of controlling the narrative, I let them take the lead. They're allowed to be quirky. They're allowed to do things their way. And if it makes me cringe sometimes (because let's be real, we've all had those "Please don't do that in public" moments), I remind myself that it's not my job to make them fit in—it's my job to make sure they know they don't have to.

Just #ShortYellowPencilGirls Living in A Neurotypical World

If there's one club my daughters and I belong to, it's the #sisterhoodoftheshortyellowpencils.

Saffy, Immy, Pen, and I? We're not just mother and daughters— we're sisters in navigating this beautifully neurospicy world. Together, we've learned to scribble masterpieces all over the walls of expectation with the tiny, imperfect pencils life hands us. We celebrate when we break out of societal molds, even as we support one another when it feels like the world is trying to dull our imprints.

This sisterhood isn't just about surviving—it's about thriving. It's about taking those stubby yellow pencils and turning them into tools for advocacy, connection, and unapologetic authenticity.

sticky note to self

Instead of being embarrassed by your kids, just seize the opportunity to embarrass them more.

They Just Keep Swimming

Parenting isn't about raising perfect kids, but this only works up to the point at which they escape the womb. I've learned it's about raising kids who feel loved, understood, and free to be themselves. All three of my daughters are proud advocates for disability rights, autism acceptance and mental health.

These days, Saffy is in England with her fiancé Alex—both on spectrum, both advocates—and she volunteers with the local neurodivergent community while they build their life together. Immy is thriving in her career and finding her place in the world. Pen is a dedicated Chinchilla mum, navigating her final year of high school with joy, courage, and compassion in her heart.

I've stopped trying to make them ride bicycles they were never meant to ride. Instead, I'm celebrating how we all thrive together when we are allowed to function in the environment we work in best, in short yellow penciled unity.

Here's to letting go of unrealistic expectations and embracing the glorious spectrum of humanity—one fish, one bicycle, and one breakthrough at a time.

#shortyellowpencilRX—Your Daily Dose

What part of your personality have others tried to change that's actually become your greatest strength?

Page Turner

So that's neurospicy parenting—my life of beautiful chaos with three yarn balls who didn't fall far from this loom. But what happens when #shortyellowpencilsisters whose brains work in gloriously tangled ways talk to each other? We're about to hike through a spaghetti trail dialogue between me and my neurospicy girlfriend—complete with metaphors, tangents, interruptions, and made-up words that make perfect sense to us. Fair warning: Neurotypicals may experience confusion, disorientation, or the sudden urge to make a flowchart.

RANDOM DOODLE SPACE

Noodled Thoughts...

Fully Marinara'd

Chapter 16

We Wander Together
(And Admittedly We're Getting Lost,
But Now It All Makes Sense)

You know what some people say about us
#shortyellowpencilgirls?

"You always make it about yourself."

"You monopolize conversations."

"Can you just let someone else talk?

People call us narcissistic. Self-centered. Bad listeners.

But here's the construction behind the chaos—we don't live to hijack conversations. We are all about building #relatablepost bridges.

When someone shares their pain and we respond with "Oh my gosh, me too! Here's what happened to me…"—we're not stealing their spotlight. We're showing them they're not alone. We're saying, "I see you because I've been there."

The ADHD brain connects through parallel experience. We don't offer distance and platitudes. We dive into the mess with you. But to people who don't speak our language? It looks like we're making everything about ourselves. That misunderstanding? It's exhausting. It makes you wonder if maybe they're right. Maybe you ARE selfish. Maybe you DO talk too much.

Until you meet someone who speaks your language. Then everything changes.

Let me introduce you to Heather.
She's a neurospicy journalist, author, a fellow ADHD warrior, and one of the founding members of the #sisterhoodoftheshortyellowpencils when I started sharing my journal sticky notes ten years ago. Talented, creative, and neurospicy to the core. She is a suicide survivor who has walked through seasons of self-harm as she navigated her mental health journey—and she is still here, still healing, still choosing life.

For a decade, Heather has been on the perch of my #shortyellowpenciled heart which is now taking shape in my greater mission—to give the neurodivergent community Prescriptive Humor, Practical Perspective, and a Place to Belong.

sticky note to self

Spaghetti conversations aren't scattered—they're comprehensive connecting points covered in sauce of ESP-laden understanding.

That third one—a place to belong— that's what this chapter is really about. Because when Heather and I talk, something extraordinary happens: we finally don't have to translate ourselves.

When Neurons Collide: A Love Story Told in 127 Interruptions
Let me show you what I mean.

When Heather and I recorded a conversation for this book, it went exactly like you'd expect two neurodivergent brains to communicate:

Keys on carabiners (she clips hers to her pants; I clip mine to my bra)—mismatched socks (she gave up 15 years ago)—grocery shopping (our husbands GPS us through stores) —cooking disasters (fire department birthday candles; instant potato glue)—organizational systems destroyed (Ortega sauce in the wrong spot)—my manuscript being "touched"—are we narcissistic? (no—we build bridges)—we're both secret arsonists—parenting while neurodivergent—finally being understood.

Fourteen topics. Maybe three finished sentences. Forty-five minutes.

And somehow—SOMEHOW—we both knew exactly what the other person meant.

Straight Lines vs Spaghetti

Neurotypical conversations—a straight piece of linguini. Topic A—Topic B—Topic C. Everything connects logically.

Neurodivergent conversations—spaghetti in a blender during an earthquake.

And here's the thing—when someone speaks your language, the spaghetti makes perfect sense.

When Heather mentioned Ortega sauce being moved in her pantry, I immediately connected it to my manuscript being "touched" by an editor who doesn't understand how my brain organized it.

A neurotypical person would say, "Wait, how did we get from condiments to your book?"

Heather said, "OH. That's it. That's the whole problem right there."

She didn't need a map to follow my brain. She just trusted the connection was there—because her brain makes the same kinds of leaps. The connection point was the sudden panic—loss of control to someone else who is organizing it—how can anyone else not see that?!

The Text That Said Everything

After we hung up, my phone buzzed.

Heather: "Is this the LONGEST running relationship in terms of work and friendship? Because you GET me and I get YOU. I'm forty-four and I never had that before. SO MUCH PEACE because you get it."

Peace.

That's exactly what it is.

Not the peace of someone fixing you or organizing you orteaching you to stay on topic.

The peace of someone understanding you exactly as you are.

The peace of interrupting and having it feel like collaboration instead of rudeness.

The peace of making a weird connection and having someone say "YES! I see it!" instead of "How did we get here?"

The peace of not having to apologize for how your brain works.

The peace of finally coming home
to people who speak your language.

Trying vs Understanding

I have wonderful neurotypical
friends who try hard to understand
my chaos.

When I tell them about my survival systems, I get:

"That's interesting!"

"Have you tried [organized solution]?"

"Why don't you just [simple solution that misses the point]?"

They're being kind. They're trying to help.

When I tell my Heathers, I get:

"SAME."

"Obviously you made glue."

"Wait until you hear what I set on fire."

One is trying to understand from outside the window.

The other is sitting on the couch next to me in the chaos.

Both are love.

What This Means For You

Here's your takeaway:

Stop apologizing for how you communicate.

You're not monopolizing the conversation when you share your story. You're building connection.

You're not being narcissistic when you say "me too." You're offering solidarity.

You're not talking too much when you interrupt with excitement. You're collaborating in real time.

The people who label you as "self-centered" or "bad listener"? They don't speak your language. And that's okay—but it doesn't mean you're doing it wrong.

Find people who speak your language.

They're out there. In neurodivergent spaces. In ADHD groups. In autism communities. In the #shortyellowpencilRX Facebook group where we gather and make perfect sense to each other.

You'll know them because:

Your interruptions feel like collaboration, not rudeness

Your tangents are interesting, not annoying

Your "me too" stories build bridges instead of stealing spotlight

You feel SEEN afterward, not exhausting

Trust your spaghetti brain.

The connections you make? They're real, even if other people can't see them.

The tangents you follow? They lead somewhere meaningful, even if the path looks chaotic.

The way you communicate? It's not broken. It's just a different language.

And when you find people who speak it too, everything finally makes sense.

We Wander Together

Heather and I wander through conversations like we're exploring unmapped territory.

We get lost sometimes. We forget where we started. We end up in places we never intended to go.

But we always end up exactly where we need to be—with a deep sense of understanding.

You don't have to keep translating yourself to people who will never quite get it.

Find your spaghetti friends. The ones who follow your tangents. The ones who say "SAME" instead of "interesting." The ones who make you feel like you can finally stop performing normal.

Because the feeling of being understood—really, truly understood—after a lifetime of being told you talk too much?

That's not just nice.

That's healing.

That's home.

#shortyellowpencilRX—Your Daily Dose

Who are your spaghetti friends—the ones who let you wander through every tangent without getting frustrated? Write their names here. Then text them a random thought right now and watch the magic happen. And you might want to join the #shortyellowpencilRX Facebook group. We speak spaghetti fluently.

PAGE TURNER

In just a few page turns our journey through these copious amounts of words will be over, but not until we've taken a deep dive into our divinely-designed DNA. Because here's what I've learned—sometimes the bugs in our system aren't glitches at all. They're features. Wonderfully, purposefully haywire that connect us to people, to purpose, and to an Artist who thinks our particular brand of chaos is exactly what the world needs.

RANDOM DOODLE SPACE

Life may not be full
of waterfalls & magic ponies,

but you can't
make me stop believin' it.

Chapter 17

Heavenly Haywired
(and Divinely On-Purpose)

If there's one universal truth about technology, it's that nothing ever works perfectly. At least not in my house. Just when you think your laptop is running smoothly, it freezes right as you're about to hit "save" on that document you've been working on for three hours.

Here's a theory I've been developing in my hodge-podge, crazy-socked headspace: maybe—just maybe—we were designed with a few bugs in our wiring on purpose.

I used to think I needed to be debugged. Fixed. Upgraded to the latest version of Functional Adult. I'd see those shiny people with their color-coded planners and matching socks, and think, "Wow, their manufacturer really got the wiring right."

Meanwhile, I'm over here with my neural circuits firing like a Fourth of July celebration gone rogue. My thoughts zooming at warp speed, occasionally taking sharp left turns into anxiety, or sometimes stalling out completely in the parking lot of depression.

If I ever had dinner with the Queen (rest her soul), I'd probably get hair caught in my mouth during our introduction, followed immediately by showing her what I call my "Tooth Fountain." It's my great party trick—just pair a prominent front tooth gap with nervous saliva glands, and you'll understand why I'm self-watering.

> sticky note to self
>
> I'm the kind of girl that needs to take time to focus on the simple things ... like navigating obvious walls and low ceilings.

But what if those bugs in our system aren't glitches at all? What if they're features?

System Crash to System Cash

Remember when computers would crash all the time? The "blue screen of death" was a regular visitor. Your work would vanish into the digital void, and you'd be left staring at a cryptic error message that might as well have said: "Computer go bye-bye now."

I've had plenty of blue screen episodes in my life. Days when my mental operating system just shuts down completely. When my emotional hard drive seems corrupted beyond repair.

But here's a beautiful twist: Those system crashes often lead us to discover workarounds we never would have found otherwise.

The bugs in our system force us to become more creative, more resilient, and more empathetic toward others experiencing similar glitches.

It's Time to Unite

My fellow #shortyellowpencilsisters, here's what I've learned after years of trying to function in a world designed for perfectly sharpened No. 2 pencils: In the realm of refined art, I'm a classic Monet. From far away, you might be deceived into thinking I'm this glorious meadow of painted oils and brushed blooms. But pull me in close, and you'll see all the crazy blops of paint that just don't line up.

Sometimes my thoughts move so fast it's hard to tie them down. I get depressed or anxiety-ridden when I can't keep up. But I realize that it's not good or bad, it's just the real vulnerability painted into this Monet soul.

So here's my radical proposal: What if we stopped trying to throw away the random blops of art that our lives create—the nonsense to others that we've scribbled over—all that wiring we'd like to have debugged?

What if my racing thoughts aren't a glitch in my system but a gift that helps me connect ideas in creative ways?

What if your emotional sensitivity isn't something to be trained out of us but a superpower that allows you to notice things others miss?

I'm not saying we shouldn't take our meds, go to therapy, or develop healthy coping strategies. Self-care matters! But what if we did those things not to "fix" what's broken but to optimize what's already valuable?

If I can do anything with my life-print, it's to give the world a greater understanding of what the face of mental illness, the sculpt of what the neurodivergent brain can look like ... and it looks a lot like me:

A little girl who loves Jesus and coloring pictures for His fridge. An "another brilliant idea" squirrel hyped up on espresso. A professional writer and editor who uses an unholy amount of em-dashes and ellipses. A girl who rocks hair rollers as an accessory (I've actually worn them to church just for fun.)

Live Authentically. Love Extravagantly.
In a world that filters everything to perfection, there's revolutionary power in showing up as your authentic, haywired self.

Here's the universal truth I've discovered: The things that make us feel broken often become our greatest strengths when we stop fighting them and start working with them instead.

Those racing thoughts? They can become innovation. That heightened sensitivity? It can become empathy. That tendency to overthink? It can become wisdom.

An irrational fear probably has deep roots in a great imagination—EVEN WHEN IT DOESN'T FEEL LIKE IT. There is a brain underneath all of that terror that is extraordinary at creating vivid, detailed, emotionally real experiences. That's an amazing complex human mind, even though it's terrifying.

You see though, these things are like being given the gift of a beautifully painted wild unicorn with wings. You have to first bridle your unicorn so it doesn't shish-ka-bob you when you take the saddle—and that takes conscious redirection, sometimes meds, and a desire to understand how you work best, along with self-advocacy.

What if you embraced your particular combination of wonderful weirdness and said, "This is exactly who I am. And that's not just okay—it's valuable."

Not despite your bugs—your haywiring, but because of them.

The world needs fewer mass manufactured pencils and more colorful, slightly bent, beautifully and wonderfully chewed ones.

#shortyellowpencilRX—Your Daily Dose

Think about a time when your brain's "divine wiring" made you feel like the odd one out. How did that experience eventually connect you to someone else?

And so, my #shortyellowpencilsisters, may your unique wiring illuminate paths others cannot see, may your bugs become treasured features, and may you always find beauty in the extraordinary design of your wonderfully haywired self.

 **42** 

The Haywired Origins Story
(Random Sub-Chapter Plot Twist for All The Sci Fi Geeks on this Page)

Okay, so... we've danced around a lot in this book.

We've talked about psychiatric wards and ADHD brains and puddles-that-aren't-oceans and finding your people and all the practical sticky note wisdom I could fit onto these pages.

But there's been something underneath it all. A framework. A… foundation, maybe? The thing that's been quietly holding this entire chaotic mess together.

It's my "42"—some of you might go "Ah. Yeah. That makes sense." And some of you might go "Wait, THAT'S what this whole thing was about?"

In the sci-fi novel *Hitchhiker's Guide to the Galaxy*, author Douglas Adams never told us what the Ultimate Question was. He just gave us "42" and let us wonder.

I've been throwing back silent respects to him for sixteen chapters—giving you the strategies without telling you how I finally embraced the fullness of my DNA that is uniquely me. What my version of "42" actually is.

Next chapter? I'm going to tell you.

Not because you NEED it to use any of this. (You don't. Everything works on its own.) But because I can't write a book about being honest with myself and then…not be honest with you.

It's the thing I've been most afraid to say out loud.

The thing that feels too personal. Too specific. Too … much?

But it's also the thing that's been saving my life this whole time.

So if you're curious—if you want to know what a #shortyellowpencilgirl does when she finally finds her answer to life, the universe, and everything—turn the page.

If not? That's okay too. You can stop here with the tools and understanding you've gained from the pages you've dogeared ahead of this one.

But for those of you who are still here.

This is my real PAGE TURNER

This is my "42."

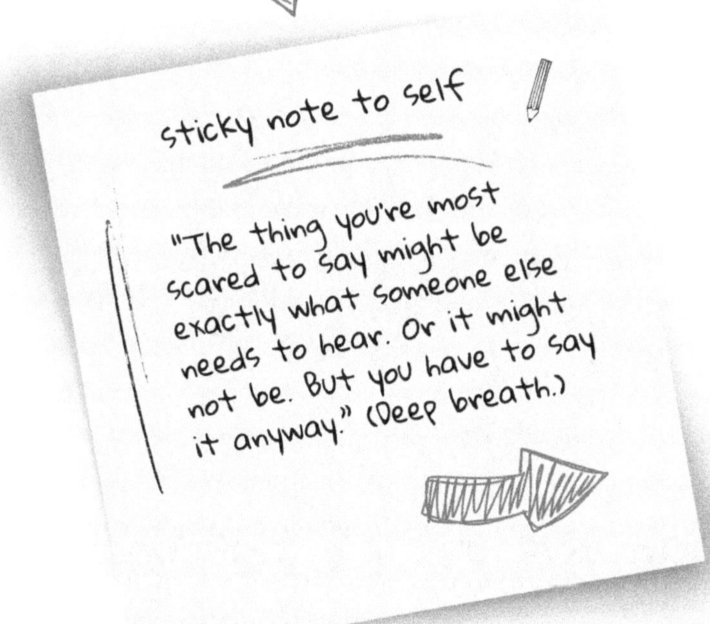

you can dive out of this book now,

or swim a few more pages...

Chapter 17

Because I Have to Say It
(But You Don't Have to Read It)

As you know, I grew up knowing about God. Church on Sundays. VBS summers. Memorizing Bible verses in Sunday school. But knowing about God and knowing God's love for me deep down in my heart were two very different things.

For years, I treated faith like a performance review. Good behavior = God's approval. Bad behavior = disappointment from the Almighty. My relationship with God looked less like a relationship and more like an employee desperately trying not to get fired.

Then the psych ward happened.

There I was—broken, medicated, scribbling on sticky notes with a chewed-up yellow pencil—and for the first time in my life, I had absolutely nothing to offer God. No good behavior. No impressive résumé. No "look how together I am." Just me, a mess, asking if He was still there.

And here's what I discovered—He'd been there the whole time. Not waiting for me to get my act together. Not disappointed in my breakdown. Just...there. Loving me in the mess. Loving me through the mess. Loving me because of the mess, because it finally cracked me open enough to let Him in.

That's when I understood grace. Not as a concept, but as a reality. Grace isn't God tolerating your mess until you clean it up. Grace is God meeting you in the mess and saying, "You're still Mine. You've always been Mine. Your worth isn't based on how well you're holding it together."

And here's what happened when I finally came to understand how much God loves me: all of a sudden, nobody else or what they were doing mattered. Not in a "I don't care about people" way, but in a "I'm finally free from needing their approval" way. When you know you're loved by the Creator of the universe, other people's opinions lose their power. Their judgments can't touch you. Their expectations can't control you. You're free to just... be.

The Cliff Story (The Full Version)

I told you earlier about standing on that cliff in Colorado, contemplating whether my story should end there. What I didn't tell you was what happened next.

I felt these words punch my heart with an unmistakable request: "Step back."

And then: "You'll have a story to share I'm not finished writing."

I could've dismissed it as my brain playing tricks. Lord knows my brain was doing all kinds of things at that point. But I knew that Voice and it was distinct—different from all the other voices screaming in my head. It felt like...love. Not conditional love. Not

"I'll love you if you get better" love. Just pure, relentless, "I'm not letting you go" love.

I stepped back from the cliff.

Three months later, I was in the psych ward, and that same Voice was still there. In the chaos. In the medication fog. In the moments when I couldn't even form coherent prayers. He was there. And now, more than 13 years later, part of the story He continues to write in me is now laid in penciled scribbles, sticky notes, laughter and tears—the pulled in close heart of who I am in 5-D, thrown in the ink of over 250 TMI'd pages of this book. A book over 52 years in the making—no makeup, no titles, no pretense, no perfection—from a beloved #shortyellowpencilgirl just like you.

What This Means for You

Here's what I need you to know, whether you believe in God or not. You are not too broken for love. Your struggles do not disqualify you from belonging. Your brain chemistry does not diminish your worth. Your worst moments do not define your identity.

For me, that truth is rooted in Jesus—the God who became human, experienced suffering, and loved people at their absolute worst. The One who looked at broken, messy, complicated people and said, "You're Mine."

If you've been waiting for permission to bring your whole mess to God—including your mental health, your medications, your diagnoses, your doubts—here it is. He's not afraid of any of it. He's not waiting for you to get better before He shows up. He's already there, in the middle of your mess, loving you exactly as you are.'

The Invitation (If You Want It)

If you're tired of carrying everything alone, there's Someone who wants to help. Not by magically fixing your brain chemistry (therapy and meds still matter), but by walking with you through every hard moment and reminding you that your worth isn't measured by your mental health.

If you're ready to start that relationship, it's as simple as telling Jesus:

> "I'm tired of doing this alone. I believe You died for me and rose again. I believe You love me—mess and all. I need Your help. Come into my life. Walk with me through this. I'm Yours."

That's it. No perfect words required. No "getting your life together first" needed. Just honest conversation with the God who's been waiting for you to stop performing and start receiving.

What Happens Next

This isn't magic. Your brain chemistry won't necessarily change. Your struggles won't disappear overnight. But you'll have Someone walking with you who never gets tired, never gives up, and never stops loving you—even on your worst days.

And here's the beautiful part—God uses short yellow pencils. He takes what the world sees as inadequate and writes the most incredible stories. Your mess? That's not a disqualification. That's your testimony waiting to happen.

And when you finally see yourself through His eyes—really see the value God places on you, and the overwhelming sense of belonging His love creates—everything shifts. Because belonging to God means we actually belong somewhere. And sometimes that somewhere isn't where we've been knocking ourselves trying to fit in all along.

If You're Not Ready (And That's Okay)

If this chapter isn't for you, that's completely fine. But if you ever change your mind? God's not going anywhere. He'll be right there, waiting with open arms, ready to meet you in whatever mess you're in.

Prayer for All of Us (Believers and Skeptics Alike)

May you know you are loved—completely, relentlessly, without condition. May you find people who see your mess and stay anyway. May you discover that your worth isn't tied to your productivity, your mental health, or your ability to hold it together. May you embrace your inner short yellow pencil— worn down, heavily chewed, and still writing beautiful things. And may you always remember, you are not alone.

Welcome to the Sisterhood

Whether you prayed that prayer or not, you're still part of the #sisterhoodoftheshortyellowpencils. Short, yellow, heavily chewed, and still making our mark on the world—writing some beautiful chaos together.

Next Steps (If You Want Them)

If you just made this decision: Tell someone (accountability helps). Find a loving church home that understands mental health (yes, they exist). Start reading the Bible , even if it's a verse a day (try starting with the book of John). Keep talking to Jesus honestly about everything. Stay connected with your therapist and meds (faith and mental health work together).

Remember, God isn't afraid of your questions, your doubts, or your need for medication. He often works through these tools to bring healing.

You're precious. You're loved. You're never walking alone.

Now go rock the #shortyellowpencilsister you are—like the beautiful boss lady you were always created to be. I'm in your cheering section!

#shortyellowpencilRX: Your Daily Dose

Sit in the quiet and allow yourself to fully feel the love of Jesus completely cover you. That's all. Just take at least one minute and sit with Him.

Stay in the Loopy

Join the #shortyellowpencilRX Community

shortyellowpencilRX.com

On Social: @shortyellowpencilRX

Prescriptive Humor

Practical Perspective

A Place to Belong.

The umbrella community for all humans and friends of humans navigating mental health and neurodivergence with humor, honesty, and hope.

All amazing brains welcomed.

I'm just sitting here Lassoing in

Amber's Random Rodeo of Bronco-Bucking Brilliance

**If you're in crisis right now
don't delay!**

**US: Call or text 988 (Suicide & Crisis Lifeline—24/7)
International: findahelpline.com**

**You are not alone.
Your life matters.
Please reach out.**